grow your
creative
BUSINESS

Turn your Passion into Profit
as a Creative Entrepreneur

Dedicated to. . .

The many creatives who have been our inspiration in writing this book and helping us become "Creativepreneurs". Without them, this book would not exist.

grow your *creative* BUSINESS

Turn your Passion into Profit
as a Creative Entrepreneur

Mark Burwell
Cheri Larson

Published by Evolutions Business Group

First Printing: 2018

ISBN-13: 978-1-4507-3481-3

Evolutions Business Group
De Pere, WI 54115

Design & Layout: Cheri Larson

For more information on books, workshops, coaching and keynote addresses, visit: www.growacreativebiz.com

CONTENTS

Introduction 9

Acknowledgements 10

About the Authors 11

Forward 12

CHAPTER 1: WELCOME TO THE WORLD OF ENTREPRENEURSHIP

BUILDING A COMMUNITY OF ENTREPRENEURS 14
WHY SMALL BUSINESS IS SO IMPORTANT 15

CHAPTER 2: THE JOURNEY TO BECOMING A CREATIVEPRENEUR

CREATING SUCCESSFUL CREATIVEPRENEURS 18
CREATIVEPRENEUR ASSETS 19-20

CHAPTER 3: SCULPTING YOUR CREATIVE BIZ PLAN

PREPARING A BUSINESS PLAN 22
THE JOURNEY TO A CREATIVE BUSINESS PLAN 23
CRAFTING YOUR OUTSIDE ENTERPRISE TEAM 24
COMMITMENT TO GOAL SETTING 25
BUSINESS START-UP CHECKLIST 26
WHY IS PLANNING IMPORTANT 27
MAKING THE RIGHT CONNECTIONS 28

CHAPTER 4: CRAFTING YOUR STATEMENTS

POSITIONING YOUR BUSINESS 30
YOUR VISION STATEMENT 31
CRAFTING YOUR VISION STATEMENT 32
YOUR MISSION STATEMENT 33
CRAFTING YOUR MISSION STATEMENT 34

CHAPTER 5: PAINT A CREATIVE BUSINESS CANVAS

PAINTING YOUR BUSINESS CANVAS 36
GROW A CREATIVE BIZ MODEL CANVAS 37
ELEMENTS OF THE CREATIVE BIZ MODEL 38
COMMUNICATING THE VALUE PROPOSITION 39

CHAPTER 6: VISUALIZE YOUR MARKET LANDSCAPE

DISCOVER MARKET OPPORTUNITIES 42-43

BURWELL'S TREND RESPONDING MODEL 44

CREATING YOUR PRODUCTS AND SERVICES.. 45

DISCOVERING YOUR IDEAL CUSTOMER 46

FOCUS ON ONE PERSON ONLY 47

CHAPTER 7: BUILDING YOUR BRAND

BUILDING YOUR UNIQUE BRAND 50

POSITIONING TEMPLATE 51

BRANDING ELEMENTS.. 52

BRANDING STYLE GUIDE 53

BUILDING YOUR BRAND EXPERIENCE 54

CHAPTER 8: PROMOTING YOUR BIZ

WEBSITE FUNDAMENTALS.. 56

QUICK & EASY SEO TIPS 57

SOCIAL MEDIA CONTENT & SCHEDULING... 58

SOCIAL MEDIA CONTENT TIPS 59

SOCIAL MEDIA - FACEBOOK 60

SOCIAL MEDIA - PINTEREST.. 61

SOCIAL MEDIA - TWITTER 62

SOCIAL MEDIA - INSTAGRAM 63

SOCIAL MEDIA – LINKEDIN 64

EMAIL MARKETING FOR CREATIVES 65-68

5 SIMPLE PR STRATEGIES.. 69

PUBLIC RELATIONS FOR CREATIVES 70-72

CRAFTING YOUR PRESS KIT 73

ANNOUNCEMENT NEWS RELEASE SAMPLE 74

TIPS STYLE NEWS RELEASE SAMPLE 75

BUILDING YOUR BUSINESS WITH A BLOG... 76

CHAPTER 9: DISTRIBUTING YOUR PRODUCTS OR SERVICES

BRICKS OR CLICKS 78

CREATIVE SALES OPPORTUNITIES 79-81

EVERYTHING ETSY 82

CHAPTER 10: MAKING IT ALL WORK

DEFINE YOUR BUSINESS STRUCTURE 84

LEGAL ISSUES FOR A CREATIVE BIZ 85

WHAT IS INTELLECTUAL PROPERTY 86

PEOPLE COUNT 87

MOTIVATING YOUR TEAM 88

INSURING YOUR BUSINESS 89

TYPES OF INSURANCE... 90

HOUSING YOUR BUSINESS 91

LOCATION EVALUATION 92

CHAPTER 11: ALL ABOUT THE $$$

FINANCIAL MANAGEMENT... 94

UNDERSTANDING A BALANCE SHEET 95

PROFIT AND LOSS STATEMENT 96

CONTROLLING OPERATING COSTS.. 97

FINAL TIPS FOR MANAGING EXPENSES 98

THE ART OF PRICING 99-100

CHAPTER 12: GROWING YOUR CREATIVE BUSINESS

VENTURING 102

SURVIVING GROWTH 103

BUYING OR SELLING A BUSINESS 104

DEALING WITH INVESTORS 105

THE 5 C'S OF CREDIT 106

CHAPTER 13: RESOURCES

SOCIAL MEDIA SIZES 108

CREATIVEPRENEUR RESOURCE TOOLKIT 109-113

SAMPLE DONATION FORM 114

CHAPTER 14: TOOLBOX & TERMS

BURWELL'S 3 DOZEN REVIEW TIPS 116

SOCIAL MEDIA GLOSSARY... 117-120

BUSINESS TERMS 121-123

We have used the Mandala symbol throughout this book. The word Mandala (pronunciation *mon-dah-lah*) means "circle". A Mandala represents wholeness and was used by ancient people to represent the whole universe.

The design of the mandala is visually appealing; allowing you to calm your mind, releasing outside thoughts until you are able to reach a higher awareness. This allows your busy mind to take a break while your creative mind is allowed to run free.

We felt this was a meaningful symbol for creative entrepreneurs as you explore your opportunities and develop your direction in business. You will notice a variety of mandala designs throughout the book. Take the time to relax, enjoy them and unleash your creativity!

Introduction

Congratulations on deciding to explore the opportunities in starting, expanding, or in some cases, saving your creative business.

We will help **empower** you to believe in yourself, teach you strong business practices and provide tools and resources to help you succeed.

As creatives, it's easy to feel overwhelmed and unsure of the direction you need to take. That's why you need a compass to help guide you.

You are taking the right step in preparing yourself for creativepreneurship:

- This book serves as a compass including business and marketing practices, concepts, trends and strategies.
- Along the way, you may need to hire professional help or seek additional training and counseling.
- By preparing your creative business canvas, your journey will give you additional paths to explore.
- This book will be your companion and guide in visualizing and creating your business.
- Remember...your canvas needs to change as your business changes.
- Never be afraid to ask for help.

The journey will be yours...and we will share your struggles as well as celebrate your successes. This book and our online tools will help guide you in the right direction.

An impressive list of participants have graduated from our workshops and become successful entrepreneurs, changing the landscape of their various communities. We are happy to have you join us on this journey!

~Mark Burwell and Cheri Larson

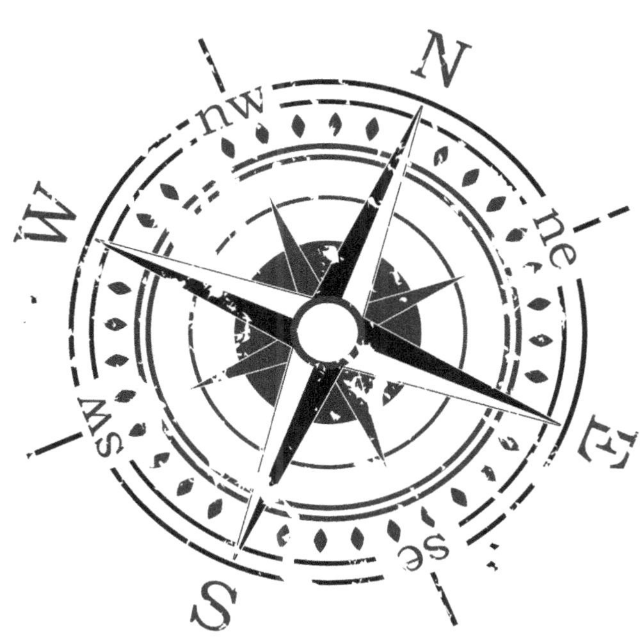

This book is dedicated to the many creativepreneurs that provide our communities with a vibrant heart and soul.

In the process of writing this book, we have met many amazing entrepreneurs who are making a difference each day. They shared stories of their passion and struggles in finding their way in a world that does not always value the arts or creative endeavors.

It is our hope that through learning, sharing and connecting, we can make a difference to those searching for a way to turn their passion into profit.

Throughout our careers we have found that giving back is vital to our sense of accomplishment and well being. Many of the creativepreneurs we've encountered are doing exactly that. Thanks to all of you who are making a difference in creating more beautiful communities for us to enjoy!

We would also like to thank our family and many friends for their support as we embark on another new journey. Your encouragement means the world to us!

Thanks also to our team of mentors and guest presenters who have offered their advice, connections and dedication to our mission.

Mark Burwell & Cheri Larson

*Around the world, people view the **butterfly** as a symbol of endurance, change, hope, and life. We see it as a part of the transformation that we make as we become entrepreneurs and evolve into the creative souls we were always meant to be.*

Mark Burwell

As an award-winning serial entrepreneur, mentor, author, business architect and senior executive, Mark draws on over 35 years of working with over 3,000 entrepreneurs in launching and growing their businesses. As CEO, he built a Midwest fashion apparel firm into a nationally recognized menswear retail, catalog and internet business.

He has led as National Director of Urban Hope Entrepreneur Center (known as E-Hub) since 2002 where he has been the architect for creative programs and entrepreneurial concepts in practice. Mark received the Innovation Champions Award from the University of Wisconsin Innovation Center for his work in advancing innovative entrepreneurship in Wisconsin. The University of Wisconsin Stout presented him with the Distinguished Alumni Award for his career, business and civic achievements. He was honored as Wisconsin's Small Business Advocate of the Year by the U.S. Small Business Administration for creating a level playing field for small business.

As president and owner of Evolutions Business Group, Mark has studied, lectured and consulted nationally as well as internationally. He empowers entrepreneurs with his energy and wisdom in the understanding of their businesses, customers, and communities.

Cheri Larson

Cheri is an artist and creative entrepreneur who has launched and operated a number of successful businesses over the past 35 years.

As a marketing professional, she ran a successful advertising agency and video production firm for over 20 years. She then followed her passion for jewelry design and founded a national direct sales business in 2003, employing over 200 consultants in 28 states. In 2006, she was recognized by the Green Bay Chamber of Commerce as Entrepreneur of the Year for Azante Jewelry. She was selected by the U.S. State Department in 2010 for a cultural exchange program where she traveled to Israel and Jordan to mentor female entrepreneurs.

Cheri creates mixed media art, jewelry, and a line of eco-friendly products which she markets on her company website, Etsy and Amazon. She also teaches and consults with entrepreneurs and small businesses in marketing, branding and social media.

She encourages entrepreneurs to reach higher in developing themselves and their business. Through mentoring, teaching and creative expression, Cheri helps others to follow their passion.

Making a living as an artisan or creative entrepreneur has long been misunderstood, but this endeavor is one that has contributed to our community's culture and economic landscape since the beginning of civilization.

Our Goal:

- To empower entrepreneurs and their communities through innovation and creativity.
- To foster creativity that will build on an entrepreneur's ideas and allow them to express and use their creative talent to become community leaders.
- To cultivate and reward champions.
- To feature the arts, open and green spaces, and vibrant downtowns.
- To tap into creative talents, challenging them to be entrepreneurial.
- To encourage those in their next career path to follow their passions and foster their skills and talents.

Our youth are sometimes discouraged to become artists for fear of not having a consistent income. Our programs have celebrated many successful entrepreneurs in business services, manufacturing, health and wellness, technology, main street businesses, restaurant and hospitality, but *also* in the ARTS. We have worked with hundreds of art related businesses including many solo entrepreneurs and growth businesses.

These include:

Classic fine artists, graphic artists, commercial photographers, jewelers, architectural designers, musicians, and entertainers, apparel and clothing designers, potters, restauranteurs, chefs, creative bakers, art framers, web designers, sculptors, home decorators, urban farmers, muralists, gallery owners, laser, welding and metal artists, stylists, writers, marketing creatives and many more with a creative way of doing business.

Hundreds of jobs and viable income have made these entrepreneurs contribute to a diverse culture and community.

Grow a Creative Biz is an action-oriented program that was created as a result of working with thousands entrepreneurs in the past 15 years.

Through our understanding and long-term relationships with creatives, we are able to address the issues that most often result in business failure; emotional blocks, lack of focus and inadequate knowledge of the business mindset.

We invite you to join us on this journey to become a successful creativepreneur!

WELCOME TO THE WORLD OF ENTREPRENEURSHIP

PASSION IS A CRITICAL ELEMENT TO BEING SUCCESSFUL.

It is an attitudinal force that generates energy, creativity and productivity.

Innovative communities are vibrant when they are creatively nurturing entrepreneurship, accepting diversity, new life styles and culture.

New ideas and change are the growth engines of tomorrow. Opportunities will reside in a community that empowers people with the ability to express innovation.

Some communities are conservative. They do not reward change or innovation and are dying as a result.

- We must pay attention and create an ecosystem. This must be a vibrant downtown! Arts, culture, nightlife, music, restaurants, artists, entrepreneurs, exciting gathering spaces, churches, public places, new neighborhoods and commerce.
- We must pass the ball as a team. Organizations must become connectors and collaborate to get everyone into the game.
- We must challenge conventional wisdom and tap into young, creative talent and energy within the community.
- We must convert the negatives into the positives. Dare to be different. Don't look back at what should have been done.

What is important to entrepreneurs?

- **"Leave me alone"** (to government) - Looking for a level playing field.
- **Access to talent** - Knowledgeable and trainable workers.
- **Access to capital** - Innovative-seed capital. Need more start-up financing.
- **Networking opportunities** - "Cupiding" - is the strength of creatives empowering development.

  - Strategic alliance partners

  - Service providers

  - Resources, government

- **Infrastructure** - Local institutional and government support. High speed internet access, creative and fair developers, good streets, FedEx, etc.

"We make a living by what we get. But we make a life by what we give."

- Winston Churchill

Why Small Business is so Important

"A part of the American Dream has been that a man or woman could choose his or her own career path and rise to any height that individual desired or was capable of...provided that person was willing to pay the price...in time, in talent, in money...in whatever else was necessary to attain those goals.

Sometimes the American Dream meant opening or getting started in a small business. It is what the pioneers thrived on. It became the major vehicle for upward mobility for thousands of people from every ethnic, social, religious and educational background. It became a conduit to a better life for the poor, the immigrant and the economically deprived.

In the marketplace, small business has increased the number and types of goods and services offered. It has been a showcase for unique and varied talents, and it has enriched the communities it served. Thousands of small business entrepreneurs prosper because they provide a product or service at a quality level that cannot be duplicated by mass production or mass distribution.

Communities have recognized the varied contributions of small businesses as well as the stable jobs it offered. In small businesses, young people often found their first jobs whether part-time, after school or during vacation periods.

Americans have always needed challenges and many seek those challenges in small business. The personal need for achievement, recognition and autonomy may not be met by employment with a large company. Small business offers open-ended opportunities to satisfy such needs."

- Mark Burwell's acceptance speech as "Wisconsin's Small Business Advocate of the Year."

"The critical ingredient is getting off your butt and doing something. It's as simple as that. A lot of people have ideas, but there are few who decide to do something about them now. Not tomorrow. Not next week. But today. The true entrepreneur is a doer, not a dreamer."

– Nolan Bushnell

"The important thing is not being afraid to take a chance. Remember, the greatest failure is to not try. Once you find something you love to do, be the best at doing it."

-Debbi Fields

THE JOURNEY TO BECOMING A CREATIVEPRENEUR

"YOU HAVE SOMETHING WONDERFUL TO OFFER THE WORLD"

Learn how to Innovate, improve and persevere while you build your business.

Doing what you love and actually making money from it is the goal for most creatives. Successful entrepreneurs do not waste time on their negatives or weaknesses. They capitalize on their strengths, build on them and attract and inspire others with complimentary skills and vision.

Entrepreneurs are architects and designers of innovation. They take risks, sometimes with little profit to advance their ideas, new services or intellectual property into the marketplace.

Creativepreneurs are a select group of entrepreneurs. As "right brain" thinkers they tend to be visual, action-oriented learners. These individuals experience a disdain for the day-to-day details of business and would rather spend their time pursuing their creative endeavors. Can they still be successful in business? Absolutely.

Can entrepreneurship be taught?

Of course! The principles presented in this book are designed to meet the challenges that many creatives have when approaching the business aspect of their work. This book will provide you with practical, proven business advice and serve as a toolbox filled with resources and powerful business tools.

How do I know if I want to take this journey?

People who have the energy and passion for entrepreneurship are admired. If you are someone who is inspired by people who have made a contribution to our community and the marketplace, then you are considered an entrepreneur. However, if you are someone who is jealous of others and want to do it on your own, you may need some more skills to become an entrepreneur.

Remember, you are a unique, one-of-a-kind human being with many gifts. Your commitment and passion will have no boundaries. You may fall sometimes, but you will be successful because you will get up and continue the venture. Our intent is to open the doors to help make you a successful, self-made creativepreneur!

> ## "Be fearless in the pursuit of what sets your soul on fire."

Burwell's Definition of Creativepreneurship:

The creation of value by creatives and communities connecting through innovation, compassion, knowledge, adherence and a willingness to take a risk.

There are people that are good at **improving** what they are doing...

There are people that are good at **extending** what they are already doing...

And finally, there are people that are good at evolving creatively through **innovation.**

Creativepreneurs should THRIVE, not just SURVIVE.

By using your assets as a creative entrepreneur, you will break through the long-standing stereotype of the "starving artist".

Remember, you are creating value with your work and it's time to share it with the world. Everyone deserves to be paid accordingly for their contributions and creatives are no different.

As a visionary, innovator and leader, you have taken the courageous first steps to living an authentic creative life. Let's take a look at some of the assets needed to discover how you can be successful as a creativepreneur.

1. Core Assets of Creativepreneurship

- Self driven
- Creativity and innovation are at the heart
- Focus on creating value
- Cutting across boundaries
- Perseverance and will power

2. Key Philosophies

- Use strategy and purpose to create entrepreneurial confidence
- Think big...work small
- Believe small business is important
- Encourage diversity of thinking and ideas - embrace a new culture
- Make the most of your knowledge

"Entrepreneurial behavior is having a clear vision and then following and executing this vision."

3. Entrepreneur's Assets

- A visionary (disruptor)
- A mentor (trainer, improver)
- A general manager (operations and an everyday business mindset)
- A leader (achiever, recruit resources, community leader)
- Creatively oriented

4. Planning and Preparation

Owning and operating a small business in today's business environment is much like tending to a hive of angry bees without adequate protection. The beekeeper may avoid some bees, but others will continue to attack.

- Day-to-day activities include; paying the payroll, taxes, expenses, competition, government regulations, obtaining and retaining customers.

**"Most entrepreneurs don't study, plan or research to change to the current environment.
Be the one who does!"**

5. Other Secret Ingredients

What is it that some ordinary people possess and other lack?

- Start with your attitude
- Confidence
- Personal and business brand
- Know yourself - strengths and weaknesses
- Never underestimate yourself
- Get passionate!
- Develop the will to help and serve others.
- Always be on the lookout for opportunities

- Never give up on your dream. Be patient. Don't be in a hurry to achieve your goal. Continue to work on your business little by little.
- Do not accept incompetence
- Adapt, renew and rejuvenate or you will harden.

"I'm convinced that about half of what separates the successful entrepreneurs from the non-successful ones is pure perseverance."

-Steve Jobs

SCULPTING YOUR CREATIVE BIZ PLAN

BUILDING A SOLID FOUNDATION

"A DREAM IS JUST A DREAM . . .

A goal is a dream with a plan and a deadline."
-Harvey Mackay

The Business Plan...

A formal document that explains in detail your strategy for developing a successful business. Writing a good business plan is a must to receive financing for your business. It also helps you organize your thoughts and resources before starting the business.

There are many other reasons for you to prepare a business plan. Writing a plan forces you to consider important issues and to answer fundamental questions about your business before you actually start the business. The business plan helps you organize your thoughts as well as your resources. It helps you to communicate the specifics of your business idea to others, including business advisors, potential suppliers, major customers and family and friends. Your plan will provide a "yardstick" against which you can measure your progress during the initial years of your business. Research has shown that businesses that start with a formal business plan are considerably more likely to succeed than those that go without a written plan.

> **"There are no secrets to success. It is the result of preparation, hard work, and learning from failure."**
>
> - Colin Powell

Although there are many business plan outlines available, all have similar sections:

- Description of your business and its product/service offerings
- Documentation of the need in the marketplace for your service or product (including competitor information)
- Marketing strategies
- Production/operations plan
- Organizational structure/personnel
- Financial projections and needs

Books and/or workbooks at libraries and bookstores can provide additional guidance.

The internet also has a wealth of knowledge. It is important to not just find a template and copy your plan. Your input in your business plan will help you build your business.

The Journey to a "Creative" Business Plan

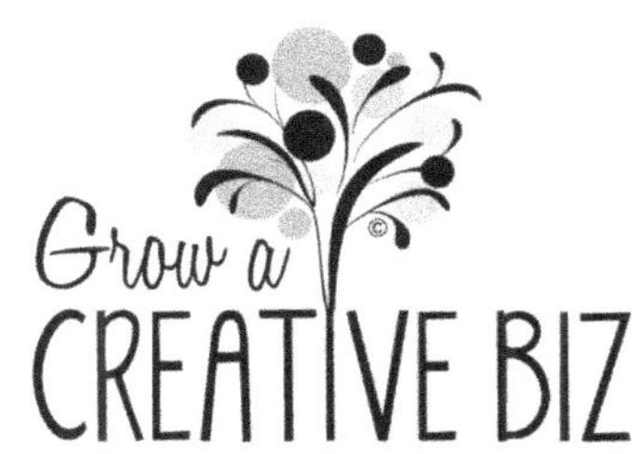

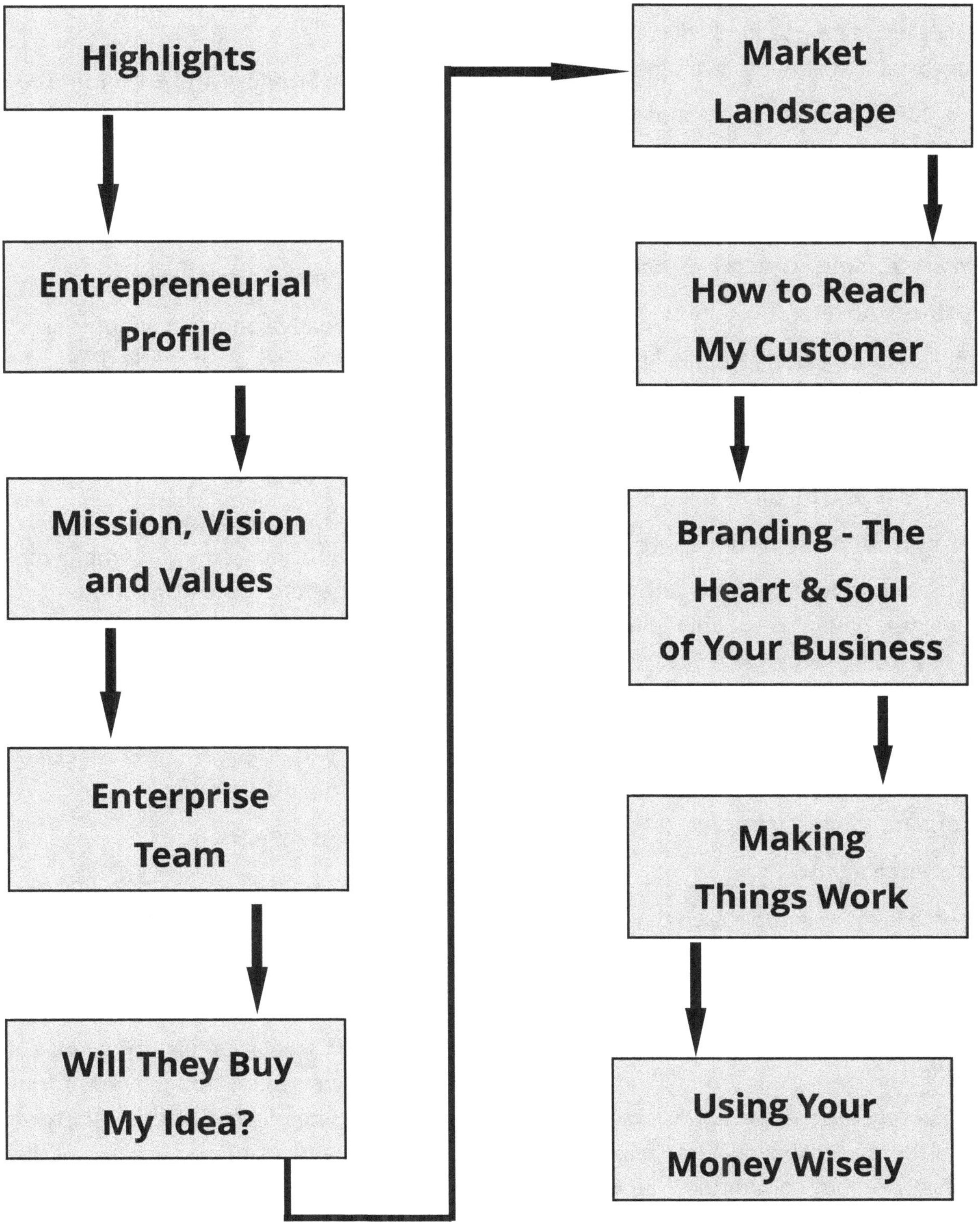
Highlights
Entrepreneurial Profile
Mission, Vision and Values
Enterprise Team
Will They Buy My Idea?
Market Landscape
How to Reach My Customer
Branding - The Heart & Soul of Your Business
Making Things Work
Using Your Money Wisely

When bringing on qualified advisors and mentors, take the time to evaluate their:

- Business ethics and philosophy
- Background success
- Experience and efficiency

Form an Outside Enterprise Team

1. Business Advisors

Example: Mark Burwell, National Director of the E-Hub Entrepreneur Center. Mark has been a business architect and mentor for over 35 years while owning, starting and operating several small and medium sized businesses.

2. Accountant or Recordkeeping

Should be used for taxes and complex cash flow analysis. If you're not able to perform basic day-to-day bookkeeping, have it done by a professional.

3. Lawyer

Used for small business issues and setting up your organizational structure.

4. Insurance agent

Insurance is more complicated than it may appear. Make sure they are knowledgeable on small business and compassionate about your concerns.

5. Banker

Interview several, feel the handshake and think of them as taking ownership in your business. Are they committed? Do they have flexibility?

6. Technical Support and E-Commerce

If you are not computer savvy, you need professionals to help you understand the basics of computer software and hardware, e-commerce and technical support issues.

7. Marketing and Social Media

You need creative people, a graphic artist and others who are skilled at marketing and social media. As you grow, marketing firms and business advisors will be helpful.

8. Human Resources

Before hiring employees, make sure you have consulted with someone with employment, tax and benefits expertise.

9. Successful Creativepreneurs

It's important to build your "tribe" of other successful creatives to brainstorm and collaborate with. Networking is especially important for solopreneurs.

10. Virtual Assistants

This is a way of having someone who is able to perform a variety of administrative support on a flexible basis.

11. Freelancers

Working with freelancers is a great way of expanding your team. You only pay for the services you need. They offer a variety of services ranging from web design, marketing, graphic design, copywriting and others.

Commitment to Goal Setting

"To attain goals we often need to expand our comfort zone and be willing to do more than what we normally would do."

Attitude is the key to success.

Winners are open to ideas and honest with themselves.

 Losers are unaware of what is happening and closed to new opportunities.

Leaders turn problems into excitement and are long term thinkers.

We must do the best we can.

Knowledge is a specific human resource.

- Knowledge is not found in books – books contain information
- Knowledge is the ability to apply what your teachers have given you
- Having talent is only a starting point

"People who feel good about themselves produce good results. Commitment is your greatest asset."

"Survive"

- To remain alive or in existence
- To continue to exist

"Thrive"

- To grow vigorously
- To prosper
- To progress toward or realize a goal

Goal Setting:

- Write down your goals
- Agree on them or reestablish them each time you reach them
- Think and live them each day
- Pick a goal that is worth the price you have to pay
- Devote yourself to the hard work that it takes to win
- Be willing to take the risk to save the joy of winning or reaching your goals
- Believe in yourself
- Focus on what is important
- Lead by good example
- Look for a better way
- Challenge current expectations
- Risk making changes

Here is a resource that can streamline your startup process. Though the precise list of needs may vary with your industry, size, and specifics of your business, there are many tasks that all businesses of any shape or size will have to check off their "starting a business" checklist.

___ Do a self and market assessment.

___ Prepare a creative business plan or business model.

___ Estimate your start-up costs.

___ Search the internet for a domain and business name.

___ Identify your paid and unpaid advisors.

___ Open a business bank account.

___ Choose an accountant to do taxes and prepare, review and explain financial statements.

___ Research your vendors and suppliers.

___ Obtain your EIN #.

___ Obtain your Sellers Permit.

___ Look at other regulatory or licensing requirements.

___ Site location, landlord background, leasing.

___ Check local ordinances.

___ Look at insuring your business.

___ Review all employment issues before hiring, including payroll processing.

___ Look at external financing and compare

- Bank
- Credit cards
- Lines of credit
- Credit card processing
- Bank deposits

___ Review technology software and hardware needs.

___ Complete your Vision, Mission & Positioning statements.

___ Prepare your marketing and social media plan.

Planning is a process that helps you reach your goals and objectives.

Day-to-day planning is part of your operations and management. It includes financial, marketing, employee and customer needs. This should be one year at a time.

Strategic planning is beyond one year and up to three years. It deals with the business industry, the current business economy and environment.

Long term planning should deal with succession planning as well as financial loan repayments up to five years and beyond.

Spend at least 10% of your time on planning, innovation and research.

"Work ON your business and not just IN your business! "

Importance of planning:
- To keep you one step ahead of your competition
- Lets you research the future trends and opportunities
- Lets you get input and follow up with your customers and employees

- Lets you act and not react
- Provides a framework for communication
- Take time to "crunch your numbers"
- Lets you prepare for growth or downturn. You must be flexible and revise the plan, goals and budgets.
- Lets you have a smooth transition or succession in your future.

Does your right-brain need a little push to get you in the planning mode? Pick up a beautiful new planner or art journal to help you get inspired and put your thoughts to paper. Sometimes a visual inspiration helps trigger the left-brain into action.

"Cupiding©"

Entrepreneurs giving back unselfishly to their communities by working peer-to-peer, connecting and matchmaking to build successful co-habitable businesses.

This meaning also signifies that giving back comes from the heart and is a true condition of the free enterprise system. Giving back can be done through time, resources, skills and connections.

Creating Social Value Connections

Making connections with non-profits or other organizations to address social responsibility as citizens is an important benefit of being a creative entrepreneur. Profit + social value equals a "double bottom line" and is a form of social enterprising. It is going above and beyond what traditional entrepreneurs and businesses deliver...it is a true movement that has created mini-heroes in our purpose of building communities. These social enterprisers play a vital role in our future. In addition, we now see "triple bottom liners" which includes profit + social cause and now the eco-environment.

Much of this social innovation has opened up doors to creating several opportunities which include:

- Marketing avenue in public image
- Employee pride and community giving

- Various forms of sales distribution channels by using non-profit volunteers and efforts.

It is a true strategic way to connect ("cupid") the non-profit sector and entrepreneurial sector to create social value.

We need to become "participants" and not "spectators." Community leaders cannot guarantee success or prevent failure. However, it is their responsibility to provide the encouragement, necessary tools and knowledge to succeed.

As creativepreneurs we must support and patronize small businesses or they will fail to exist.

CRAFTING YOUR STATEMENTS

MISSION & VISION
POSITION

"IF YOU CAN'T WRITE YOUR MESSAGE
IN A SENTENCE, YOU CAN'T SAY IT
IN AN HOUR."

-Dianna Booher

Begin the Journey of Trust

All business plans start with a **Vision Statement**, which is a picture of time to highlight what you want to accomplish and what you will look like.

Next is your **Mission Statement**, which defines the purpose of your business. It communicates your value proposition to customers.

While designing your business model marketing plan, the **Position Statement** is the key element. This describes how you will be perceived. It needs to be crafted with your brand. It must be trusted and have unique characteristics. How will you communicate it to your customers. You will work more on your Positioning Statement in Chapter 7.

"Positioning is how you differentiate yourself in the mind of your customer."

Realize now is the right time and opportunity to reposition your business.

Remember these important points in mapping your positioning:

- Minds lose focus
- Minds need to develop trust
- Minds hate confusion
- Minds are emotional

Positioning helps make your marketing plan take direction and stay lean. It is how you want to be seen.

Positioning is all about the niche. The higher the uniqueness, the higher marketing value to stay lean.

Positioning replaces the top-down communication with a side-to-side, peer to peer approach.

By co-creating you are unleashing people to create and take action.

Broaden the pond - don't force advertising. Use the drip, drip concept.

"Many of life's failures are people who did not realize how close they were to success when they gave up."

-Thomas Edison

Your Vision Statement

To ensure everyone associated with your business knows the goal of the company, it is important to have a clear **Vision Statement**. This is the place where you get to describe your vision, your way! The vision statement is a picture of the business in a future time in terms of its likely physical appearance, size, activities, etc.

WHAT

- Products or services or both? How many?
- What is your company image: What will the company be known for?
- Owner's role: What is your role? How will you spend your time?

WHERE

- Business: Local, regional, national or international?
- Customers: Where are they? What cities, states, countries?
- Business Operations: Headquarters, sales offices, manufacturing

WHO

- Customers: Who are they?
- Strategic Alliances: Who can you partner with?
- Advisors: Who can provide professional and strategic advice?

WHEN

- When will this business be operational?

WHY

- Why am I creating this business?

HOW

- Financing, culture

What are my benefits to having a Vision Statement?

You must have a means to accomplish your vision. It gives you and your employees a target or goal to focus upon when operating daily. After reading the two statements below, which team would you rather play for?

- *"The vision of the team is to be the best football team that we can be."*
- *"The vision of the team is to be this year's Super Bowl champion."*

The second example has very clear definition of where the team is going. The sense of purpose is strong and the players have a common thread or goal that runs through each of them.

 If you give your employees a sense of purpose that is as strong as that, they will follow you anywhere.

Crafting Your Vision Statement

Step 1: Crafting Your Vision Statement

Within the next _________years, grow ____
(company name)

into a successful ____
(Local, regional, national, international business)

____
(Type or description of business)

providing ____
(Description of product and/or services)

to ____
(Description of your customer)

Step 2: Write your Vision Statement.

____

____

____

____

____

____

____

____

What is a Mission Statement?

The nature of a business is often expressed in terms of its **mission,** which indicates the purpose of the business. For example, "To design, develop, manufacture and market specific product lines for sale on the basis of certain features to meet the identified needs of specified customer groups via certain distribution channels in particular geographic areas."

The mission statement describes the purpose for which your product, service or business exists. It communicates in a few words the company's focus and what is being provided to customers.

A mission statement is an enduring statement of purpose for an organization that identifies the scope of its operations in product and market terms.

What are my benefits to having a Mission Statement?

Businesses write mission statements so clients will know what type of business they are, so employees know what to expect from the business or to direct future decision-making.

A mission statement will help a company make consistent business decisions, motivate associates and owners, build organizational unity, integrate short-term objectives with longer-term goals and enhance associate-to-associate and associate-to-customer communication.

How to Create and Use a Mission Statement

Mission statements have become a part of business culture. You can think of the mission statement as a cross between a slogan and an executive summary. Just as slogans and executive summaries can be used in many ways, so too can a mission statement. An effective mission statement can complement all the other good things you do.

Step 1: Crafting Your Mission Statement

The mission of ____
(Your Company name)

is to provide ____
(Description of product and/or services)

to ____
(Description of your customer)

These ____
(Description of product and/or services)

will ____
(Description of how the product and/or services will benefit the customer)

Step 2: Write your Mission Statement.

____

____

____

____

____

____

____

PAINT A CREATIVE BUSINESS CANVAS

VALUE PROPOSITION

"ACTION WITHOUT VISION IS JUST PASSING TIME.

Vision without action is merely daydreaming, but vision with action can change the world. "
-Nelson Mandela

The New Rules of the Game.

We cannot adapt quick enough with just business plans to survive the accelerating rate of changes in the marketplace.

The New Canvas:

- Customer: The customers have changed, they are better informed. They want fast service! They want transparency.

- The Internet: It serves as a platform to launch a new business. It also helps us connect, shop, entertain, and communicate 24/7/365.

- Social Value: Is here to stay - It is a way to distinguish yourself from the competition.

- Technology: Is changing every second and is widely available. It is cheap. We can use technology at no cost such as Skype, Word Press and more.

- Hitting the bull's eye in relevance to your target customer is your winning game plan. We are overloaded with information. Just in time delivery makes our buying decisions easier. Learning to design, mobilize and implement your business model then manage, adapt and response to this new economy will help you succeed as an entrepreneur.

Evolutionary Barriers:

The first is shifting of assets that are needed due to operational or marketing expenses. The second is cognitive...the inability of owners, managers and staff to change to the current business models.

How do you Overcome these Barriers?

Construct maps of business models. The new evolutionary process is a discovery driven process of experimentation. This planning helps you create a culture that encourages employees to the objectives, "what if." The core element and logic of business model revolves around the firm revenues and costs, its value proposition to the customers, and avenue to capture that value. In the end, the business model can serve as a vehicle for innovation as well as a source of innovation.

As markets develop, companies compete by focusing on adding:

- Features
- Reliability
- Convenience
- Speed
- Commodity on price

Developing business models prevents this situation, where you chase and package products with technology for example. Instead, your implementation of a new business model is to deliver a more compelling customer value proposition, thus growing revenue and profits.

Grow a Creative Biz Model Canvas

The Market

Who is your customer or client? Identify your customer segment groups. You may have one or several.

Value Proposition

These are the unique gifts of products and services that create value to your customer segment. Does it solve a problem or satisfy a customer need?

Customer Relationships

How do you interact with the customer through their journey? What type of relationships will you build for your referral or repeat customers? This is the driving force to connecting, networking and "cupiding".

Marketing Channels

These are you way of communicating and raising awareness about your value proposition for your products and/or services. What are the customer touch points you will be using?

Delivery of Goods and Services

How will your customers reach you to receive goods and/or services? Will it be in person, a retail store, catalog, internet, etc. Sales, distribution and fulfillment are all part of the equation.

Resources and Your Enterprise Team

What assets are required to make your business work?

Key Resources can be physical, financial, intellectual, or human. These are the most important assets required to make a business model work.

Human Resources include yourself and your enterprise team. Solo entrepreneurs may need subcontractors to fill in additional resources. *Physical Resources* include facilities and equipment. *Intellectual Property* includes copyrights, trademarks and patents.

Activities

These are the most important things that your business must do to make it work successfully. Your creative product or service takes care of unique needs.

Partners/Connections

This is your network including; non-competitive alliances, joint ventures to develop new business, leveraging of volunteers in partnership with non-profits. *Note:* Many partners or resources may convert to customers.

Revenue Streams

These create the cash flow for the model. For what value are your customers willing to pay for? How much does each revenue stream contribute?

Investment/Cost/Expenses

What are the most important costs in your model canvas? You are able to design low cost structures while still delivering value, marketing, maintaining customer relations and generating revenue.

The Largest Challenge an Entrepreneur Faces is Communicating the Value Proposition.

Small businesses never seem to get enough seminars, workshops and webinars on marketing, advertising and now social media.

The biggest mistake most make is approaching promotion tactically rather than strategically.   You need to take the guesswork out of defining your target market.

Identifying your value proposition is the reason customers and clients pick your company. It is the centerpiece of communicating why people choose you.

Once you create this value you need to identify how you will reach your customer base.

Before diving into your marketing strategies you need to define your niche target audience. Hitting the target is essential otherwise you'll waste time, money and energy. This not only wastes your resources but can erode your sense of value in communicating your perceived value.

To be effective you need to identify your psychographics. These are values based on assessments of customers. They identify how consumers spend time, what work they do and what brands they buy.

Demographics describe education, sex, age, race and geographic location.

In the end you need to develop your value proposition. An effective value proposition answers the questions your target audience is wondering every time they learn of your new product or services. They ask themselves, "What's in it for me?"

Many small business start-ups think they want to appeal to all people which usually results in not being anything to anyone.

"Cultivating your value proposition in life is the way to move forward. You are the raw material of your own destiny."

-Bryant McGill

"There is a spiritual aspect to our lives - when we give, we receive - when a business does something good for somebody, that somebody feels good about them!"

-Ben Cohen, Ben & Jerry's

VISUALIZE YOUR MARKET LANDSCAPE

MARKET OPPORTUNITIES
TREND RESPONDING
YOUR IDEAL CUSTOMER

EVERY DAY IS A JOURNEY,
WITH NEW THINGS TO DISCOVER

*"And suddenly you know it's time to start something
and trust the magic of beginnings"*

Getting Your Special Piece of the Pie

Understanding the market you want to target is probably the most important issue your business needs to succeed.

Understanding words like demographics, segmentation, psychographics, behaviorial targeting, and market analysis are sometimes confusing to entrepreneurs.

Simply stated. . . Who is your Customer?

Let's start by looking at two segments to target:

Business to Business (B2B)

- They are usually larger acccounts
- You have to get it right first because you won't get as many chances to have additional clients after you've reached your target.
- Big businesses are easier to find due to data that is available.

Business to Consumer (B2C)

- Consumer groups are the hardest to dissect and analyze. Their data is harder to find and evaluate.
- Brands are important.
- They purchase small amounts.

In the last decade, entrepreneurs began to recognize that being technology driven was just not good enough. What came of this? The Customer-Driven Movement.

First . . . understand what your customers want.

Growth creativepreneurs struggle with:

- Bad data collection and analysis
- Not identifying the right growth target markets
- Improper marketing & branding
- Missed opportunities & channels
- No business model to fit the new business generation

"Entrepreneurs and small business owners are always looking for the silver bullet. Unfortunately, there is no crystal ball. You must be continually observing and listening to the marketplace."

To discover new markets and grow your core markets you need to discover the idea of "Outcome Driven Innovation."

Listening to the voice of the customer has been the mantra for the last three decades. This voice tends to slow down the creative process because our customers are not the best qualified to know the best solutions. We need to get better input to solve the customers true value proposition. Many times our messaging channels fail to show the true value proposition.

Defining Your Customer Markets

In mature markets, companies find it more difficult to discover unique opportunities and as a result they often compete on price, eroding company profits by moving toward being a commodity seller.

One way to avoid this is to be more creative by looking at the underserved customer markets.

Who are these markets?

There is always a group of customers who are more demanding than the rest. They are the "PROSPECTS". They are underserved in the value proposition. They want more and are willing to pay for it.

Markets that should NOT be targeted.

These I will call the "SUSPECTS". They may require excessive service while demanding lower prices. You benefit from understanding this segment and avoiding them.

Research, research, research . . .

Take the time to see what's out there. The internet allows us to find out rather quickly if our "unique idea" is really unique or has been out there for years. Market research is the simplest way for entrepreneurs to keep up with market trends and maintain a competitive edge by sizing up your business opportunity. Market research can be carried out at various stages of a business life cycle, from pre-launch and beyond. Having a greater understanding of your marketplace from the very start will enable you to create a sound business strategy to establish and grow your brand into one that's better than the competition.

Blue Ocean Strategy© for Creativepreneurs

Blue Ocean Strategy© is a marketing theory from a book published in 2005 which was written by W. Chan Kim and Renée Mauborgne, professors at INSEAD and co-directors of the INSEAD Blue Ocean Strategy Institute.

The authors argue that lasting success comes not from battling competitors but from creating "blue oceans"—untapped new market spaces ripe for growth.

There is a call today for creativepreneurs to be relevant and rethink the marketplace. In a blue ocean, competition is irrelevant because you can create your new concepts, art or rules. Blue oceans are wider, deeper, and unexplored portions of the marketplace. Swimming in the red ocean is floundering in a competitive existing market space. Blue ocean space is an uncontested market where you create and capture new demands or needs.

As a creativepreneur, use Blue Ocean Strategy to become an innovator and find new untapped growth potential that awaits you and your business.

The Creative Biz Model Canvas will help you change your business mindset to adapt to the rapidly changing market.

Burwell's Trend Responding Model© will provide you with a solid guide to building revenue and developing a creative growth strategy.

The percentages shown are dedicated to your costs, energy and resources. It will help serve as a guide to balancing your product or service offerings during turbulent, competitive or abundant times.

10% New Innovative Products or Services

Seek out new, exciting, creative items and services to offer your customers.

20% Trend Responding

Create a feeding frenzy of must-have items, such as gifts, apparel, activities or experiences.

40% Basic Products or Services

These are your "bread and butter" staple items with a solid price and value.

10% Related Products or Services

These are your add-ons that complement your basic staple items. They can be add-on

---

BURWELL'S TREND RESPONDING MODEL©	
10%	New Innovative Products or Services
20%	Trend Responding in Industry
40%	Basic Products or Services
10%	Related Products or Service
10%	Promotional/Value Oriented
10%	Bundle/Tier Pricing

---

services such as delivery, warranty, safety, maintenance and training. These items help to build customer loyalty.

10% Promotional/Value Oriented

This is an area to allocate excess inventory, matching your competition and increasing your customer base.

This area also provides opportunity money for additional revenue streaming.

10% Bundle/Tier Pricing

This increases the amount of sales per purchase and allows you to be creative with your offering. Don't bundle jobs on an hourly rate. Tier pricing on service or products over a given period of time to cover your less demanding times. An item with purchase incentive is also a way to introduce new items.

"Remember, people don't buy products or services. They buy your value proposition via benefits, needs and experiences."

It's important to not only be a creator, but a "Trend Responder". You need to identify your customers trends and lifestyles before you can spend money on creating, launching or marketing your products or services.

"You must continually be aware of your customer's changing inspiration, needs and demands."

Learn to be focused, flexible and always aware of what's happening in the marketplace. To be a successful entrepreneur, you must be a successful trend responder.

Building customer loyalty and keeping them satisfied is a true asset. But if market share is slipping and marketing is not working, brand relevance comes into play. Categories or sub categories are part of keeping your product line ahead of the curve.

Innovate and Take Risks

As an entrepreneur, you can't afford to always play it safe. Think about creative opportunities to:

- Expand the boundaries of your existing brand category.
- Carve out a new sub-category.
- Develop new technology.
- Design a new method of distribution.

Stay Inspired and Think Outside the Box

How can you solve problems with your products or services? What innovative solutions can you design to shake up your industry.

What additional add-on products or services would keep your customers coming back for more?

Observation, Intuition and Research are the Keys to Developing Your Offerings

It's important to listen to your target market - read articles, blogs, magazine articles, online conversations, talk to people in and out of your industry - anything that will help you to discover what your target market really needs. Use this information to build a better product or service.

"Just remember to listen to your target customer, but don't always take their advice literally."

The one mistake entrepreneurs make over and over again is responding to what their customer asks for without taking the time to explore if this makes sense for their business. Listen carefully, then do your research. Remember to always keep focused on the "big picture" of how you want to grow your creative business.

Before you can begin a marketing strategy, you need to know EXACTLY who your customers are. By developing a Customer Profile, you'll have a good idea of who your ideal customer is, how you can reach them, and most importantly, why they will want to do business with you. Your ideal Customer Profile or "buyer persona" is made of many characteristics that will help you to reach them and speak to them in the most effective way possible. In the following exercise, we'll focus in your one ideal customer. By honing in on this one person, it forces you to dig deeper into understanding their habits, preferences and what drives them. This information can be the difference you need to nano-target your customer and not waste precious time and money targeting the wrong person.

"Your ideal customer is the one person who won't be able to resist what you offer"

Demographics

Social and economic characteristics:

- Age
- Gender
- Occupation
- Income
- Education
- Family structure
- Where do they live

Psychographics

Attitudes, behaviors and aspirations:

- Hobbies
- Personal Values
- Religious Views
- Favorite movies, music, books
- Leisure time activities
- Favorite places to eat
- Places they travel
- Personal style/clothing choices
- Spending habits

You need to dig deeper than using broad demographics, like women 25-54. You have to truly understand your customers habits, preferences and needs so that you can attract then and serve them better.

In other words, figure out "what makes them tick". That extra bit of digging into your buyers persona, makes the difference between speaking to the crowd and speaking to your targeted customer.

Example:

Jane is a 45 year old married professional woman with no children. She works for a non-profit and earns between $50-$60K per year and enjoys shopping for unique decor items for her home. She loves classical music, NPR podcasts, "House of Cards" on Netflix and shopping with friends at small boutiques. She is a frequent online shopper primarily from Chico's, White House Black Market and Target. She spends weekends with with her husband or friends. They enjoy going out for dinner at trendy restaurants and listening to live music. Her style is eclectic and she fills her home with modern furniture and antiques. Her favorite magazine is Real Simple. Once a year she takes an international vacation to a warm weather location. She's influenced by friends she respects and strong women leaders. She supports social justice causes and considers herself politically liberal. Her personal style is a bit bohemian and she enjoys handmade jewelry and bright colors.

EXACTLY who is your Ideal Customer. . .

1. What does she do for a living?
2. Does she have hobbies or leisure activities?
3. How does she use the internet? (music, social media, shop, blog, share photos)
4. What media does she consume? (magazines, news, blogs, TV shows)
5. What is her style (clothes, accessories, hair)?
6. Where does (and doesn't) she shop?
7. How does she spend her free time?
8. Who influences her (friends, political leaders, artists, actors, etc.)?
9. What types of food and drink does she like?
10. Does she enjoy travel? Where?
11. Does she have pets?
12. Is she married, single, divorced?
13. Does she have children? How old?
14. What kind of home does she live in?
15. What causes does she support?
16. What are her splurges?

"Let excellence be your brand. When you are excellent, you become unforgettable."

-Oprah Winfrey

BUILDING YOUR BRAND

ELEMENTS OF BRANDING
POSITIONING
STYLE GUIDE

"THE CUSTOMER DOES NOT CARE HOW
MUCH YOU KNOW UNTIL THEY KNOW HOW
MUCH YOU CARE."

-Damon Richards

"If you don't define your brand, your customers will decide for you."

Your brand is quite simply who you are and what you stand for. The purpose of building a strong brand is to inspire trust with your ideal customer so that they will want to work with you or buy from you. With the right tools, you will influence their perception and drive their buying habits.

GETTING STARTED

BRAND MESSAGE

What do you have to communicate to your potential customers? This message should express your values and goals, which may evolve over time. This should be a single sentence. Here are a few examples.

Nike: To bring inspiration and innovation to every athlete in the world.

Starbucks: To inspire and nurture the human spirit - one person, one cup and one neighborhood at a time.

H&M: More fashion choices that are good for people, the planet and your wallet.

BRAND POSITIONING

This is the process of positioning your brand in your customers mind. You need to determine and portray your brand with specific attributes that are different from the competition.

POSITIONING STATEMENT

This statement defines the compelling benefit or reason to buy. Unlike mission statements, a positioning statement shows where and how you fit into the market among your competitors.

POSITIONING TEMPLATE

For *(target audience)*

who *(description of need or opportunity),*

BRAND/PRODUCT is a *(defined category)*

that *(provides key benefit).*

Unlike *(competitor/alternative),*

BRAND/PRODUCT *(provides key differentiator)*

EXAMPLE POSITIONING STATEMENT

Grow a Creative Biz is for creative entrepreneurs who want to build a successful business.

Grow a Creative Biz provides the training needed to quickly start and grow your business. By helping you develop a business model and providing a variety of tools and resources, you'll learn from a variety of entrepreneurs that have been on your journey.

Unlike other workshops, online courses or books, we base our advice on our personal entrepreneurial endeavors and the experiences of over 900 entrepreneurs that have graduated from our program.

POSITIONING STATEMENT

POSITIONING STATEMENT

This statement defines the compelling benefit or reason to buy. Unlike mission statements, a positioning statement shows where and how you fit into the market among your competitors.

POSITIONING TEMPLATE

For ____

(Target audience)

who ____

(Description of need or opportunity),

BRAND/PRODUCT is a ____

(Defined category)

that ____

(Provides key benefits)

____

(Provides key benefits)

Unlike ____

(Competitor/alternative),

BRAND/PRODUCT ____

(Provides key differentiator)

____

(Provides key differentiator)

EXAMPLE:

For eco-friendly consumers, who want to cut down on waste and save the environment, EarthSAKS are reusable shopping bags that are strong, portable, long-lasting and cut out waste. Unlike other giveaway bags or cheap alternatives that don't hold much or fall apart after only light useage, EarthSAKS strong rip-stop nylon holds up for thousands of uses and is washable and small enough to fit in a purse or pocket.

Brand Image

Here are five key assets to help show others what your brand is all about:

- Name & Logo
- Slogans & Taglines
- Color Palettes
- Typography
- Tone & Voice

These are the key items needed to promote your brand in person and online.

Name & Logo

These are the basics. Because logos are the visual asset that get used and shared the most, take the time to have a professional logo designed to reflect your brand. Make sure you have these versions available:

Suggested Files:

- High-res EPS file for print
- Med-res TIFF for office use
- Low-res JPG or PNG for web

Suggested Versions:

- Color
- Black and White
- Reversed Out
- Favicon icons

Slogans & Taglines

Mostly used in advertising, these can be easy-to-remember phrases that help customers to remember you.

Examples:

Target: Expect more. Pay less.

BMW: The ultimate driving machine.

GE: We bring good things to life.

Tone & Voice

Your brand needs a distinct voice which expresses it's personality. Is your brand fun and whimsical or serious and authoritative?

Think of your IDEAL CUSTOMER, when you write and share your voice. If it doesn't resonate with that person . . . try again.

As you keep thinking about brand personality, think about what you want to portray. Here are a few comparisons to get you started:

- Formal or funny?
- Big or small?
- Boring or surprising?
- Reserved or outspoken?
- Stylish or classic?
- Premium or inexpensive?
- Masculine or feminine?
- Rigid or flexible?
- Charming or quirky?

BRING YOUR BRAND TO LIFE WITH A STYLE GUIDE

Once you determine your brand personality, you need to design your style around it. Start by creating design visuals that portray your personality and style. The key visual elements are color, typography and imagery.

Just as words create voice, so do the visuals. Certain colors can make you feel happy or sad, fonts can be seen as feminine or masculine, images can be dark and mysterious, or inviting and happy.

Associations and emotions should coincide with the brand. Here are a few common elements and their associations:

COLOR

Warm colors: Happy, inviting, stimulating, active

Cool colors: Calm, relaxed, serene

No color: Stark, bleak, simple

Complementary colors: Harmonious, soothing, trustworthy

Contrasting colors: Bold, active, impactful, chaotic, energetic

Saturated colors: Intense, bold

TYPOGRAPHY

Serif typefaces: Formal, trusting, mature

Sans serif typefaces: Informal, agreeable, modern

Script typefaces: Typically feminine, elaborate, special

Uppercase type: Impactful, bold, pushy

Lowercase type: Informal, relaxed

Titlecase type: Trustworthy, solid, expected

IMAGES

Images with no borders: Informal, fun, surprising

Images with heavy borders: Strong, impactful

Images with fine borders: Expected, mature, honest

OTHER ELEMENTS

Square elements: Formal, expected, mature

Rounded elements: Informal, fun, casual, modern

Alignment: Common alignments are more formal (left and justified), while right and centered alignments are more casual and chaotic

Space: More space creates a sense of organization and harmony while tightly packed elements seem cluttered and chaotic

Create a "WOW" experience for your customers!

Your brand is a reflection of you and everything you stand for. Do you want your customers to feel special when they open a package from you? Do you want to leave a lasting impression when they receive a handwritten thank you note from you?

Image is everything!

The good news is that is doesn't need to be expensive and it doesn't need to be time-consuming. It has to be heartfelt and it has to be authentic to who you are and the brand you've established. If your visual brand looks cheap or unprofessional, that's the way you will be perceived. Here are a few tips to creating a special "WOW" experience for your customers.

Always go the extra mile.

I have a friend who sells crystals and stones on Etsy. There are literally hundreds of others who sell the same product. How does she stand out and create a special "WOW" brand experience?

It all starts with her photography and product descriptions. She tells a compelling story about the items and makes it personal. She explains how the items **will make you feel.** Then when you purchase, the final piece of the brand experience is revealed. Her items are wrapped in beautiful paper, scented with essential oils and tied with vintage ribbons or yarn. A unexpected, handwritten note or vintage photo or rose petals, are included. The point is, you never know what you might receive, but it is always amazing and personally curated with love and creativity.

There are many packaging options available in the Resource section of this book. Take the time to choose packaging that is authentic to you and your brand image.

If you are in the service industry, your branding "WOW" may include a small handwritten note after you have worked with a client. Choose special stationery with a heartfelt message and you will be sure to stand out in your clients mind.

Putting the "WOW" in your customer experience.

The building blocks for any great relationship are communication. Always keep your customer in the loop on terms, delivery times, shipping and return policies. Clear communication is a great way to ensure expectations are being met. Always put yourself in the customer's shoes and provide the kind of quality experience you desire.

From the first interaction to the final delivery of product or service, pay attention to making your customer experience one that they will talk about to friends and family. This type of "cupiding" is more valuable than any marketing you will ever do.

PROMOTING YOUR BIZ

WEBSITE & SEO
SOCIAL MEDIA
EMAIL MARKETING
PUBLIC RELATIONS

"MARKETING IS NO LONGER ABOUT THE STUFF YOU MAKE BUT ABOUT THE STORIES YOU TELL."

-Seth Godin

Whatever your business, having a website is essential. Your website is the online face for your business and your brand. It's the place you will introduce yourself, tell your story and what you have to offer. If you plan on selling online, your website becomes your virtual marketplace. All your marketing, online and offline, should be directed to this central hub - your website.

Whether you are working with an Enterprise member to design your website or building it yourself, here are the key elements needed to begin.

CONTENT

- Pages
- Blog Posts
- Sidebars
- Videos
- Pictures
- Audio
- Downloadables
- Links

ORGANIZATION

- Site organization
- Site hierarchy
- Navigation
- Menus

CREATING YOUR WEBSITE

IDEA

- Purpose of site
- Call-to-Action
- User interaction
- E-commerce

DESIGN

- Layout
- Graphics
- Colors
- Photos

WEB HOSTING

- Domain Name
- Web Hosting Service
- Theme

Set up a Google My Business account

If you have a small business that relies on local customers, it's important to set up a Google My Business page and add as much detail as possible.

With the blended search results, having a My Business page could mean your small business website shows up not just in Maps but also in Google+ and the natural search results.

Ask for reviews on Google My Business page

Encourage happy customers to leave reviews on your Google My Business page. While there's no absolute proof that more reviews result in higher rankings, if you're already ready ranking well then having a lot of positive reviews can encourage click-throughs to your website.

You can also use these testimonials on your website and social media.

Build a fast, mobile-friendly website

Google is focusing more and more on mobile optimization. Their goal is to encourage website owners to provide the best mobile experience possible. They've even gone so far as to indicate which sites are mobile-friendly in the mobile search results.

Start a blog

Each blog post you write is a chance to rank for a new keyword phrase related to your business. But great content that solves your customers' problems can also build your authority as the go-to small business in your industry.

Start using Google Search Console

Google Search Console (Previously know as Google Webmaster Tools) is a great place to find data, tools and diagnostics for a healthy, Google-friendly website.

Don't rely on SEO too much

Divide your marketing time between SEO, social media, email, PR and other channels. Building your brand in whatever way you can will always benefit from your SEO efforts. People will start searching for who you are, rather than just what you do.

Using Keywords

To improve your understanding of the language even further, visit Google's Keyword Tool. Just type in a word or phrase and a page of suggested similar terms or phrases will appear. Next to each similar term, Google's Keyword Tool displays the number of global monthly searches received for it. The higher the monthly searches, the more popular the term.

This will not only help you find new keywords, it will also help to refine the language you're using and attract more buyers to your shop.

Also check out **Moz.com's Keyword Explorer** to see keyword suggestions and **SERP** (Search Engine Results Page information).

There is no real rules when it comes to what you can share on social media. It depends on your target market and your audience. If you went through the " ideal customer profile" exercise, then you should already have an idea of what content your ideal customers would like to see/read about.

Have a system. It can be an app, a printed calendar, or whatever works for you to schedule your posts in advance Get into the habit of keeping the pictures or ideas you might have during the day and that you want to post later in the same place to access them easily when it comes to scheduling. Experiment with different times and days to see what works best with your audience. Be authentic and have fun! ENGAGE! It is called "social" media for a reason... you don't want to spend too much time doing this, but it is important to spend the time answering comments and commenting on other people's feed/posts/images to establish yourself.

Scheduling

If you want to save time, you have to schedule your posts in advance. Block 1 to 2 hours on your calendar each month to prepare your posts in batch and don't think about it anymore!

Here is a list of some tools you can use to help you plan your content in advance on different social media platforms.

- Coschedule
- Hootsuite
- MeetEdgar
- Buffer

Instagram and Pinterest Schedulers

- Tailwind

Pinterest Only Scheduler

- Boardbooster

Instagram Only Scheduler

- Later
- Schedugram

"Focus on ONE or TWO social media networks at a time!"

EXERCISE:

Design a social media post for your business using of the 35 content ideas shown on the following page.

Explain who your target customer is and why this would appeal to them.

Choose two social media networks to use and explain how the posts will differ on each network.

SOCIAL MEDIA CONTENT IDEAS

- Behind the Scenes - Your Process, Workspace, Tools
- Upcoming Products or Services - Sneak Peek
- Inspirational Quotes
- Meet the Owner or Maker
- Community Involvement
- Lifestyle Product Shots
- Customer Interviews
- Ask for Questions from your Customers/Clients
- Short Videos
- Behind-the-Scenes Videos
- "Caption This" Photo
- Company News
- Profile an Employee
- Helpful Articles
- Share Breaking Industry News
- Posts About Obscure Holidays
- Event Announcements
- Hold a Photo Contest
- Share Tutorials
- Inspirational Stories or Videos
- Packaging (if you have a product)
- Charitable Posts
- Job Opportunities
- Choose a "Fan of the Month"
- Statistics or Data
- Share a Helpful Resource
- Make an Industry Prediction
- Customer Testimonials or Reviews
- A "Day-in-the-Life" Post
- Recommend your Favorite Products
- Share Random Tips
- Thank Your Fans
- Post a Photo Collage (use PicMonkey to create)
- Tell a Story or Interesting Anecdote from your Life
- See what your Competitors are sharing - then do it better!

FACEBOOK POST CHECKLIST

The most popular social media site for most audiences, Facebook is essential for small business marketing. 79% of all online adults use Facebook. When posting on your Facebook business page, make sure to post and share information that is relevant to your business or target audience. Here's what you should include in an ideal Facebook post, when applicable:

- Use photos or attention-grabbing graphics or video
- Engaging caption that promotes the post
- Call to action if necessary
- Be part of a trending topic
- Tag businesses physical location
- Hashtag

FACEBOOK HOT TIPS:

- Post tons of videos and photos - they get the most likes and shares.
- Photos also get a lot of comments, but text updates get slightly more.
- Posts that are either very short, or very long have a higher percentage of likes.
- Show some personality . . . posts with self-referential words, like "I" and "me" tend to get more likes.
- Post during peak times.

CREATIVE FACEBOOK POST IDEAS

- Book recommendations
- Company milestones
- Giveaways and contests
- Answer questions that a common customer may have
- Interview customers
- Tasteful humor or funny quotes
- Links to useful content
- Share other peoples updates
- Post questions or polls to your followers
- Recognize someone special

WHEN TO POST ON FACEBOOK:
Best Days: Thursday-Sunday
Best Times: 9am, 1pm, 3pm
Most Active Time: Thursday 1 pm

WHAT IS PINTEREST?

Pinterest is a discovery site. There are over 175 million Pinterest users (as of 2018) seeking information, advice, and inspiration on the network.

Demographics

With 175 million Pinterest users, the site's demographics are key. As Pinterest shares, "67% of Pinners are under the age of 40, a 27% jump from last year." Even more interesting? 54 percent of women aged 34 to 55 are on the site, and 35 percent of them have household incomes of over $100,000. Male users grew 120 percent in 2016.

Proven marketing success

Pinterest has influence on what people are buying. According to Pinterest, "87% of Pinners have purchased a product because of Pinterest" and "93% of Pinners have used Pinterest to plan a future purchase."

A top traffic driver

If your goal is to increase traffic to your website, look no further than Pinterest. Pinterest shares that about five percent of all website referral traffic comes from the site (second to only Facebook).

Pinterest Post Checklist

Use Pinterest to show off your products or pin photos from blog posts relating to your services. Here are the things to include in an ideal Pinterest pin, when relevant:

- Visually engaging photo, potentially with words
- Good description for search
- Appropriate hashtag
- Include your link in the description
- Share from your blog post

PINTEREST HOT TIPS:

- Use Pinterest to direct interested customers to your products and services.
- Create inspiration boards for clients, customers, and followers.
- Create boards based on products or services.
- Highlight your work or products.
- Label boards to be specific.
- Engage with users (comment, like, repin).

WHEN TO POST ON PINTEREST:

Best Days: Saturday and Sunday

Best Times: Most engagement at 9 pm,   2 pm and 2 am

At its core, Twitter has always been a network for conversation. But over time, marketers lost that connection and began using it as a mass messaging channel. Take it back to the essence and focus on creating personalized experiences and engage in conversations with your followers.

Don't underestimate the power of Twitter video. A whopping 82% of Twitter users watch video on the app. In addition to Snapchat, Instagram Video and YouTube, don't underestimate the power of Twitter Video.

TWITTER POST CHECKLIST

Twitter is a fast-paced social media channel but can be very useful for small businesses. It is good for real time customer engagement, and the retweet feature makes it easy to share relevant content or good customer comments and reviews. Here are some things to include in an ideal Twitter post, when relevant:

Less than 140 characters (Photos add characters so you may need to get creative!)

- Photo or graphic
- Engaging caption that promotes the post Call to Action if necessary
- Tag people or places
- Hashtags

TWITTER HOT TIPS:

Depending on your creative business, Twitter may not as strong of a lead generating channel as other social media sites. If you want to generate leads on Twitter, it's important to post regularly and engage with followers.

- Engage with followers who like, follow, & comment on your content.
- Retweet customer posts and reviews about your business.
- Find and follow others using Twellow or WeFollow.
- Use local hashtags to tweet events/sales/ promotions .
- Limit your hashtags—use no more than three per tweet.
- Use a link shortener.
- Tag users in a photo or graphic # .
- Tag a physical location.

WHEN TO POST ON TWITTER

BEST DAYS: Wednesday

Best Times: 12pm, 3 pm and 5-6 pm

SOCIAL MEDIA - INSTAGRAM

INSTAGRAM IS A MUST FOR BUILDING YOUR CREATIVE BUSINESS.

There are 600 million active users on Instagram every month, and every day one billion photos are liked. With Instagram, the quality of the posts are much more important than the quantity. According to Forrester Research, Instagram user interactions with brands is 400 percent higher than on Facebook and Twitter, delivering 58 times more engagement per follower than Facebook and 120 times more engagement per follower than Twitter.

INSTAGRAM HOT TIPS:

- Use popular hashtags every day of the week. These include #motivationmonday, #transformationtuesday, #wisdomwednesday
- Search for people who are mentioning your brand and use the Repost app to re-gram any brand mentions. Be sure to tag them in your posts.
- Connect with businesses using hashtags and geo-tags. Be sure to utilize the location feature on each post.
- Create a unique hashtag relevant to your business forfollowers to use and tell people to use it. A custom hashtag is worthless if no one is using it.
- Show followers what's taking place in your business behind-the-scenes using the hashtag #BTS.
- Increase visibility by liking and commenting on prospective customers' photos. If you like and comment on photos, people will check out your account and are more likely to follow you back.
- Offer exclusive content. If you're launching a new product or service on Instagram, try creating an exclusive offer and offer followers a unique code to track how effective the promotion was.

WHEN TO POST ON INSTAGRAM

BEST DAYS: Monday & Thursday

Best Times: 2am, 8-9am, 5pm

GROW YOUR BUSINESS WITH LINKEDIN

Start with your LinkedIn Profile. Reboot your profile every few months to keep it fresh, relevant and interesting. Each time you update your profile, the update is shared to your network (as long as you have this feature enabled in your settings).

The more people who view your profile, the more likely a percentage of those visitors will click through to your website or blog and learn more about you!

LINKEDIN HOT TIPS:

Build a Deep and Wide Network
One of the best ways to get found on LinkedIn is to build up your network of connections.Every new connection is an opportunity to enhance your visibility.

Always be Connecting!
Connect with clients, prospects, partners, vendors, colleagues, community leaders, fellow alumni and anyone you meet face to face at networking events or conferences. Personalize your invitations when possible.

Be Consistently Visible and Valuable
To become a go-to resource you must be visible, valuable and timely with your participation.

Focus on activities that have the potential to grab the most attention. These include media-rich status updates (links that showcase images) with compelling headlines; thought-provoking questions; comments on the status updates of your connections; and overall sharing of solid content. LinkedIn status updates are by far the most powerful opportunity to be visible and valuable with your network.

Leverage LinkedIn Endorsements
How can you receive more endorsements? Make sure to list all of the skills and experience that you have on your profile first, and then go out and endorse your connections based on your evaluation of the particular skills they showcase in their profiles. In many cases, the people you endorse will come back and endorse you for at least one skill.

Participate in LinkedIn Groups
LinkedIn Groups present a great opportunity to develop rapport with the members of your target markets and industry peers. Spend time focusing on 3-5 quality groups for the best results. Win favor with fellow group members by posting relevant and informative content.

Don't ever spam or make public sales pitches on LinkedIn and remember to always be professional.

WHEN TO POST ON LINKEDIN

BEST DAYS: Tuesday-Thursday

Best Times: 7-8am, 12pm, 5-6pm

EMAIL MARKETING FOR CREATIVES

Many people have said that email marketing's days were numbered and that it would soon become a dated technology. Despite the naysayers, email marketing is not dead. **It is still one of the most effective methods for reaching and engaging target audiences and remains the backbone of digital marketing.**

GETTING STARTED

Build a Good List

We all know that most of us get too much email these days. That's why you need to make sure people you're emailing to have chosen to hear from you. In marketing terms it's called "opting in." This means someone signed up to receive your newsletter on your website, your Facebook page, or perhaps by signing up on a list at an event.

DO NOT automatically add all of your past customers to your email list. This is big no-no and so is buying lists. Your goal is to create a list of people who *want* to hear from you. A solid list of subscribers translates to higher open rates (meaning, people actually opened and read your message) and higher click-through rates, which means they clicked on links to your items or services. Like many things in life, email lists are more about quality rather than quantity.

So how do you get those all-important email addresses? Simple: You need to let people know you have an email newsletter with valuable information, tips or specials that they want to receive. Here's a few ways to do that:

Website or Blog: If you have a website or a blog, make it easy for people to sign up on the homepage. When selecting your email service provider, make sure they provide code to easily drop a sign-up widget on your website that will integrate with your list. Set expectations as to what they'll be receiving, like, "Sign up for a monthly newsletter featuring our latest products!" or "Sign up to learn aboout upcoming events"

Facebook: If fans "like" you on Facebook, they'll *love* hearing from you via newsletters, right? Make it easy for them to sign up here by adding a sign-up link. **If you're using MailChimp, here are the instructions:**

- Log in to your MailChimp account.
- Click your profile name, and choose Account.
- Click Integrations.
- Click Facebook to open the integration details.
- Click the Page to use drop-down menu, and choose the Facebook Page where you'd like your signup form to appear.

Events: There are a few ways to gather email addresses at an event starting with a simple sign-up sheet. This works, but you still have to

enter the email address into your list. Another option is to use MailChimp's Chimpadeedoo, which allows people to add themselves to your list via an iPad or Android.

Online Stores: If you're selling on Etsy or any other online store, the About Page is a great place to add a link to your email sign-up page. You can also include a link to a sign-up page in your Shop Announcement and Message to Buyers.

Share: Make it easy for your subscribers to share your newsletters via social share buttons and a "Send to a friend" link.

WHEN SHOULD YOU SEND EMAILS?

Despite what some people will tell you, there is no perfect or best time to send. Timing is established after knowing what works best for your audience.

THE EARLY BIRD PRINCIPLE
If you schedule your emails to arrive in the early morning, you can be at the top of the email pile when folks arrive at the office. However, because smartphones have become like another appendage, people check their email earlier and earlier in the day — often long before they actually get to work.

EMAIL DO'S & DON'TS

Do incorporate your branding.

Your newsletter should feel like a natural extension of the visual brand you've created. Incorporating your logo and the typography and colors you use in your shop branding helps subscribers remember who you are and why they signed up for your updates.

Do send from your own domain.

Before you can send your first newsletter using MailChimp or another service, you'll need to set up a professional email alias, or forwarding email address, using a domain you own. If you haven't already registered a domain you should do that first. Once you have your domain, you can set up a custom email alias such as yourname@yourdomainname.com. This will be the email your subscribers will see in their inbox when they receive your newsletter.

Do offer an incentive.

Incentivize customers to sign up for your newsletter by offering something in return and being clear about what subscribers can expect. Whether you say you'll share DIY content, a free printable, coupon codes or sneak peeks at new products, deliver on your promise as soon as people sign up.

Do send an introductory email.

Waiting to send an introductory email will leave your subscribers wondering "When did I sign up for this?" and disappoint fans who check their inbox immediately after signing up expecting some special content. "That first email is crucial," Erin says. "This person has expressed interest in your shop so they're expecting it to be relevant to what the signed up for. If they think they're signing up to get coupons and they don't get that, they're going to lose interest."

Do share interesting content.

Make a list of all the different kinds of news, updates and content you could share with your new email subscribers. Some examples include:

- The launch of a new product line
- A sale or holiday promotion
- A new behind-the-scenes blog post
- A free printable or DIY
- A blog post on your favorite seasonal trends
- Details about a new collaboration
- Information about an upcoming in-person selling event

How frequently you send out your newsletter will depend on how often you have new content to share. If you're adding new products to your shop or publishing on your blog every week, then sending your newsletter once a week might makes sense. Sending a newsletter no more than once a week and no fewer than once per month is probably a good rule of thumb but try to stick to a consistent schedule.

Do encourage readers to take action.

Your goal when writing your newsletter is to encourage your readers to take a specific action, whether that's checking out your offerings or following you on social media. Email marketers refer to these links as "calls to action."

Do make your subject line clear.

To make your emails stand out in your customers' inboxes, your subject line should be clear and to-the-point — readers should be able to tell at a glance what they'll find in the email. To avoid repetition, make sure to vary your subject line every time you send an email. MailChimp offers some great tips on writing subject lines.

Do get the word out.

Once you have your newsletter set up, it's time to start spreading the word. Post on all your social media channels, encouraging followers to sign up with a clear message about what they can expect to receive from you.

Don't add emails without consent.

Rule number one in email marketing is to never add customers' emails to your list without their consent. There are anti-spam policies in place through the CAN-SPAM Act that can shut down your email services for sending unsolicited emails. Don't do it!

Don't spam your subscribers.

Your subscribers should be excited to see your newsletter in their inbox. Emailing too

frequently can quickly turn your emails into an annoyance and prompt your customers to unsubscribe. A good rule of thumb is to not send emails more frequently that you would feel comfortable receiving them.

> **Make it simple.**
> **Make it memorable.**
> **Make it inviting to look at.**
> **Make it fun to read.**
> **-Leo Burnett**

Don't appear too salesy.

The hard sell approach doesn't work in email marketing, so avoid it all costs. This kind of language can turn off your subscribers and get your emails sent to customers' spam folders. Avoid language like FREE, DISCOUNT, 50% off, etc. Those are usually filtered to spam. Better alternatives might be "an exclusive offer". Use words that allude to a promotion without using language that is likely to trigger a spam filter.

Don't forget to send a test.

Believe me, this is important! No matter how big or small your subscriber list is, you should always send yourself a test of your email before sending it to a larger group. Typos may make you appear unprofessional and a broken link might mean missed sales.

Don't ramble.

Emails should be short and to-the-point. People respond to compelling copy, colorful graphics, and videos that engage.

Don't worry about occasional unsubscribers.

One of the metrics you should keep an eye on is your unsubscription rate, or the rate at which your subscribers are opting-out of your newsletter. Unsubscribing is common and it's not necessarily a reflection on your brand or content. It might indicate that your newsletter or products are no longer relevant to the buyer. Don't take it personally, but do keep an eye on the data.

5 SIMPLE PR STRATEGIES

Many entrepreneurs neglect their public relations development strategy because they don't consider it a priority. No matter how busy you are, you can, *and must,* make time for these simple strategies.

1. USE THE POWER OF TESTIMONIALS. As an entrepreneur, testimonials are key. You can receive greater brand visibility, trust, increased SEO and the opportunity to go viral with a product or campaign.

- Encourage your users to post written and video testimonials on their social media profiles and websites.
- Offer a small reward in exchange for their honest opinions, or sponsor a competition that recognizes a random participant.

Initiating a steady flow of user testimonials is a way to let your customers do your PR work for you. Consumers trust other consumers more than brands, so you'll build your reputation naturally with the help of others.

2. MAKE YOUR PRESS RELEASES WORK FOR YOU. Press releases are a great source of external links for SEO, since they're usually posted on high-authority news sites. Press releases don't have to be one-use-only. If you're already creating and distributing your press releases on a regular basis, you can tap them for additional PR value with just a little extra time.

- Post a variation of the press release on your own website as a blog entry.

3. TAKE 10 MINUTES A DAY FOR STRATEGY. With just 10 minutes, you can scan your news feed, get an overview of what's happening and reach out to at least a handful of followers. You may not get time to answer every post but it will establish your brand as one that cares enough to make a daily effort.

4. FOCUS, FOCUS, FOCUS. Instead of trying to do twenty things with an average success rate, narrow your strategy to do one or two things with success. Don't try to build a following on five different social media profiles - instead focus on building an audience for one (with the other four on the back burner). You'll have a smaller potential audience, but the audience you end up with will be more passionate, more loyal, and enthusiastic.

5. LEVERAGE THE POWER OF INFLUENCERS. Stop spending hours a day trying to force your way into new markets.

- Cultivate friendships with a handful of influencers and ask them to help you.
- Look for an industry leader with a large blog following and ask them to post a link to your latest press release.
- If you know them well, ask them to create a testimonial for you.
- If they agree, you'll gain access to their massive following, giving you extra visibility without a significant extra effort.

PUBLIC RELATIONS FOR CREATIVES

Why do creative entrepreneurs need public relations . . . here's why:

- To find potential new customers
- To build a following for your creative business
- To encourage social media sharing
- To generate sales

The old rules of PR no longer apply. Sending a news release and waiting for a reporter to respond just doesn't work anymore. You can control the news cycle by self-publishing your own web-style press releases.

HERE'S HOW IT'S DONE . . .

Write a news story about your business. Keep your news releases regular, 1-2 per month. Don't wait for the big story, write about everything you are doing. Here are examples:

- Exhibiting at a new venue
- Selling artwork to a high profile corporation
- Donating some of your work to a non-profit
- Trips and travel associated to your business

Focus on keywords and phrases that your readers might use for searching for your product or service online. Be sure to include these in your content. Use images and try to create content that is entertaining and informative.

Publish your press release on your website and blog. Provide a predominant place for them to be archived. Keep them on your site for as long as they are relevant—in some cases years. Art buyers like to see a history or your successes.

Add Links in your press release. Your press release is an electronic document, which will allow you to add hot hyperlinks that will push readers to your website. Customize landing pages with announcements, special invitations to shows, and links to other sites where you might be exhibiting your work online for purchase. This can be done easily in Word, look under the "Insert" pull down menu for "Hyperlink".

NEWS RELEASES - You don't have to be an expert to write a news release. Follow the format shown below, check out news release formats online and if you're not good at writing, find someone who is.

- *Announcement Style Release:* Example - New business launch, new employee, etc. (see example)
- *Tips-Style Release:* Used to establish you as an expert in a certain area (see example)
- *Piggyback on Trends:* Look at what's in the news and find a way to make your company or product timely.
- *Piggyback on Holidays:* Get a list of pertinent holidays at: www.holidayinsights.com and find a holiday that your business can piggyback.

Find out what media your target market uses. This is about intimately knowing your target audience. Create your media outlet list (newspapers, magazines, online publications, blogs). Go online and find out where to send your news release or media inquiry.

Make sure you're aware of how far ahead all publications want material. You will need to send Christmas gift ideas in June if you want to be considered for a national magazine.

Basic Media Deadlines

• Monthly magazines – 6 months out

• Weekly Magazines & Major TV – 3 months out

• Local News *(Newspaper, Radio, TV)* – 3 weeks out

• Internet News – 2 weeks out

TOOLS & TACTICS

Once you've sketched out your plans for the year, it's time to consider the activities that'll enable you to achieve your objectives.

Establish a news release calendar to plan out the news releases you intend to issue throughout the year. You may need to revise this calendar as you move through the year, but it'll give you some initial structure to adhere to and help you stay focused on generating news.

Media outreach in the form of pitching reporters and placing articles is still the essence of PR, and the foundation for any PR program is a solid media list.

Publications' editorial calendars offer an excellent vehicle for planning media exposure. Researching them will enable you to identify opportunities to offer yourself as an expert source, contribute an article or even suggest a feature on your company. Once you've set your list of targets, begin contacting them as soon as possible. Most editorial outlets have deadlines several months ahead of their publication dates. Pay careful attention to the closing dates, or you'll risk losing out on the opportunity

BASIC NEWS RELEASE LAYOUT

Start with the lead which is an introductory paragraph. It should contain the beginning of the story and include the who, what, where, when, why - the how comes with the tips.

The second paragraph is a good place to put a quote. A quote is the only place where you can put subjective information. Remember to keep the release fact-based and the quote opinion-based.

The third paragraph highlights additional details about the topic and offers tips. Keep this fact based. Sentences should be brief.

Next is the tips section. Bullet points or numbers are used to explain the tips. You should include at least three tips. Keep them fact based and brief.

The last paragraph is called the boilerplate. It's usually no more than a few sentences and included details about you and your business.

WHERE TO SUBMIT YOUR NEWS RELEASES AND ARTICLES

- Media outlets and blogs your target market utilizes
- Online article publication sites (see list in Resources)
- Blogs who reach your target audience

"Tease" on your social media pages and include a link to the story.

How to Find Bloggers

While there are go-to lists of bloggers and media outlets you can use to pitch, you usually have to pay a lot of money to access them. Rather than spend money on a list that might not be relevant to you, create your own list by doing research.

One of the easiest ways to find bloggers and press to cover your products is to research who has covered your competition. List 10-15 brands that are similar to yours, then run that list through a Google search to find blogs publications that have written about them.

Pitching to Bloggers

Keep your email short and be succinct. You should only try to sell one big idea at a time. If the blogger decided to write on your topic, they will ask for all the details they need.

Do your homework. Make sure the blogger you are pitching covers news around your topic. Otherwise you will be wasting both your time and theirs. Additionally, referencing previous blog entries in your email will let them know you truly care.

Provide additional resources. At the end of your email, add a few links that might be interesting if they decide to write something about you. These links can point to full product specifications, photo galleries, or press release.

Show them you're unique. Bloggers like to stand out with their view point. By telling them why your company is different from the rest it will help them to formulate an opinion. Sharing 'secret' details that you have since only shared with that blogger will also entice them to cover your story since they have the exclusive inside scoop.

As one piece of your brand assets, the press kit is comprised of materials provided to the media that tell the story of your business or product. They're sometimes called "media kits" and are designed to:

- Introduce your products to the media
- Give journalists a look behind the brand
- Showcase your achievements
- Provide journalists or bloggers with content for future features

A media kit is typically a multi-page PDF document that you can either deliver digitally or print in hardcopy format.   Here are the core components:

COVER SHEET: Something to capture attention and introduce the brand. Think: visual and dramatic. Include your logo and tagline.

BACKGROUNDER OR FACT SHEET: A concise, one page document detailing the brand story, key players, sales channels, timeline of growth, achievements and company location. This is essentially your entire business distilled down to a single page.

BIOGRAPHY: Brief stories which provide a more well-rounded look at key players behind the brand.

STORY ANGLES OR PRESS RELEASES: Potential story lines that you develop so that an editor can quickly and seamlessly feature your brand and/or products in their publication. Essentially, you're doing the "thinking" for the editor. You pitch the story and they just need to flesh it out!

SOCIAL PROOF: Show them how press-worthy your brand is! Potential inclusions: past media mentions (i.e. press clippings), awards received, customer testimonials, etc.

IMAGES: Images should be print-ready, high-resolution images, which means a minimum of 300dpi. Include a good headshot, a photo of your workspace or studio, and a photo of you in the creative process.

CONTACT INFORMATION: Make yourself easy to reach by including your phone, website, email, and social media handles.

TIP: If you're looking for a pre-made template where you can simply plug in your information, media kit templates are available on Etsy.com and CreativeMarket.com

> ## "If your stories are all about your products and services, that's not storytelling. It's a brochure. Give yourself permission to make the story bigger."
>
> - Jay Baer

FOR IMMEDIATE RELEASE

Eco-Friendly Product Launch. . . Going Green in Green Bay

MARCH 31, 2011 - GREEN BAY, WISCONSIN – Green Bay entrepreneur Cheri Larson announces the launch of EarthSAKS, a new line of eco-friendly reusable bags. Products include a reusable shopping bag, made from strong, rip-stop fabric, that folds into a compact carrying pouch. Additional products include mesh produce bags and recycled cotton tote bags with clever quotes.

"My goal is to help eliminate plastic, one bag at a time," says Larson. "According to the EPA an average America family uses over 1,000 plastic bags per year. An estimated 12 million barrels of oil is required to make all the plastic bags we use in the U.S. every year and only 1 – 2% of those bags ever get recycled. Those figures convinced me to ditch the plastic and go reusable, " Larson stated.

EarthSAKS are currently available at several retailers in the Green Bay and De Pere area, as well as through the Green Girls Market website. Larson also hopes to promote the bags as an alternative fundraiser for schools and non-profit organizations.

Cheri Larson is the founder of Green Girls Market (www.greengirlsmarket.com), a business that produces a line of reusable shopping bags, organic skin care products, and products for green living. Larson has over 25 years experience in marketing and entrepreneurship. Winner of the 2006 Green Bay Area Chamber of Commerce Entrepreneur of the Year award, Larson is passionate about teaching others simple ways to "green" their environment.

For additional information, visit www.greengirlsmarket.com

Contact: Cheri Larson, Founder cheri@greengirlsmarket.com

Hi-resolution product photos and samples are available upon request.

FOR IMMEDIATE RELEASE

Make Every Day Earth Day - 10 Small Changes That Make a Big Difference

APRIL 1, 2017 - GREEN BAY, WISCONSIN – As we approach Earth Day on April 22, people are more aware than ever that lifestyle changes are inevitable in this new green economy.

"By making a few small changes, we can collectively make a big difference." That's according to eco-living expert, Cheri Larson, founder of Green Girls Market, who shares these tips on making your household a little greener.

1. Do away with one-use plastic and paper bags and carry reusable bags.
2. Kick the bottled water habit. Carry your own refillable water bottle.
3. Use environmentally friendly household cleaners or better yet, make your own with simple things like lemon juice and baking soda.
4. Use reusable containers to carry your lunch and ditch plastic sandwich bags and aluminum foil.
5. Reuse your plastic bread bags and cereal bags. They make great lunch bags.
6. Be creative with gift wrap – use newspaper, comic pages or decorate old paper bags.
7. Buy food products grown locally. This saves transportation costs, offers you fresher foods and helps sustain local farmers.
8. Buy a solar powered battery charger and use rechargeable batteries for your gadgets.
9. Donate usable items instead of throwing them away. Landfills are full of items that many other people could use. Think before you throw.
10. Compost vegetable and fruit scraps. These make fabulous food for your garden.

"Remember, every little bit helps. We may not all be able to afford a new hybrid vehicle, but a few simple changes in our lifestyle can reap huge rewards for our environment," says Cheri Larson.

Cheri Larson is the founder of Green Girls Market (www.greengirlsmarket.com), a business that produces a line of reusable shopping bags, organic skin care products, and products for green living.. Larson has over 25 years experience in marketing and entrepreneurship. Winner of the 2006 Green Bay Area Chamber of Commerce Entrepreneur of the Year award, Larson is passionate about teaching others simple ways to "green" their environment.

For additional information, visit www.greengirlsmarket.com

Contact: Cheri Larson, Founder cheri@greengirlsmarket.com

Hi-resolution product photos and samples are available upon request.

Getting Started

Start by selecting your name and custom domain. Select a template or theme by using Wordpress or Blogger as your blog website host. Link your blog to your website. A blog is just another part of your brand, so remember to keep it consistent with the rest of your visual branding with colors, style and fonts.

Be sure to use lots of keywords that your target market may be searching for. Share what you're working on and your process. Tell your story. Show readers what you do and how you do it.

Posting content regularly on your blog helps you rank higher in the search engines which helps potential customers find you more easily.

Establish yourself as an expert

Blogs are wonderful tools to help people establish themselves as experts in a field or niche. We all have expertise to share with others. If you're able to produce great content on your blog and/or have a unique point of view on the topic, you'll be a successful blogger and will develop a following of loyal fans who become customers.

What should you write about?

Start by thinking about questions your customers regularly ask you. Help them to understand what you do and the benefits your product or service offers. Use your blog as a way of giving people an "inside look" at your creative process.

How often should I blog?

It's more important to have quality over quantity when writing a blog. With that being said, consistency is important as well. Post on a regular basis for the most engagement with your customers. Some creatives post once a day, once a week, and others once a month. Do what works for you, but do make a commitment and schedule it on your calendar.

Make friends and have fun

With practice and a little effort, you can easily build your base of fans and followers. As you become known as an expert in your niche, you can inspire, encourage and help your followers make a difference in their own lives.

Make money from your blog

Blogging may well become your passion but you can also make money with your blog. In fact, many bloggers are able to make a living from blogging. There are many ways to monetize your blog. You can place ads and receive compensation from companies by promoting their products and services. Or you can sell your own digital products and merchandise.

"One of the best ways to promote your business and connect with potential customers and buyers is to write a blog."

SALES OPPORTUNITIES

BRICKS OR CLICKS
CREATIVE SALES OPPORTUNITIES

"DON'T FIND CUSTOMERS FOR YOUR
PRODUCTS, FIND PRODUCTS
FOR YOUR CUSTOMERS."

-Seth Godin

Distribution channels are a key element in your entire marketing strategy — they help you expand your reach and grow revenue.

To create a good distribution program, always focus on the needs of your customers or clients.

If your customers prefer to buy online, create an e-commerce website and fulfillment system and sell direct. Also consider selling to another online retailer that can offer your product on their own sites.

Will your distribution be through Bricks or Clicks?

In other words, will you be selling in a physical location such as a retail store or through "clicks" as in online shopping. As a B2B or a B2C business you can sell through a single distribution channel or through multiple channels. Here are just some of the ways for you to consider the distribution of your product or service:

- Wholesaler/Distributor
- Direct/Internet
- Direct/Catalog
- Direct/Sales Team
- Consultant
- Dealer
- Retail Store or Office
- Sales Agent/Manufacturer's Rep

- Social Enterprising - Distributing your product or service through a partnership with non-profits and volunteers to solve a community need.

All of these will determine:

- Sales operations
- Packaging
- Shipping & delivery
- Staffing hours
- Pricing

Evaluate how your customers need to buy

Your distribution strategy should deliver the information and service your prospects need. For each customer segment, consider:

- How and where they prefer to buy
- Whether they need education and training to use your product or service
- Whether they need additional products or services to be used along with yours
- Whether your product needs to be customized or installed
- Whether your product needs to be serviced

> **"The purpose of a business is to create a customer who creates customers."**
>
> - Shiv Singh

Teaching Classes, Workshops or Retreats

Teaching classes or workshops can be a great way to monetize your creativity. Selling art is another benefit of teaching workshops. Whether you hold them in your studio or a public location, make sure to display a wide selection of your art for attendees to appreciate while they're learning. Holding workshops will also help increase your overall exposure and profile in the arts community. Below is an example of a floral artist using Facebook to promote a workshop.

Online Classes

If you're somewhat tech-savvy and enjoy sharing your skills with others, online classes can be a wonderful way to monetize your expertise. Once you've identified you're target audience and topic, created an outline, and have an idea about how your course will work, it's time to launch. (Yes, before you've created the content!) One of the best things about e-courses is that you can open registration before you've created all the content. This ensures that you'll have paying customers before you invest too much time in creating the course.

You can use something as simple as a sales page with a PayPal "Buy Now" button, or create a product listing using shopping cart software like Big Cartel. The most important thing is that you make it clear and easy for individuals to register and that you provide details of the course; when it starts and ends, what they'll be learning, and what they'll need to participate.

When creating your content, focus on being yourself, sharing your passion, and having fun. Students signed up for your class not just because of the topic, but because YOU are the teacher. Relax, enjoy the process, and focus on sharing the best you have to offer, because that's really the secret to creating a standout course.

Digital Products and Downloads

Creative Market dubs itself as "a platform for handcrafted, mouse-made design content from independent creatives around the world." You can sell stock photography, fonts, graphics and more. You set your own prices and earn 70% of the sale price.

Rather than just sell through the websites mentioned above, you can also sell your digital downloads directly to your patrons through websites like Etsy.

Licensing Artwork

ArtLicensingInfo.com is a virtual library on art licensing. Check out titles like How to be a Press-Friendly Artist, How to Find an Art Licensing Agent, How to Find, Interact and Work With Manufacturers Who License Art, and How to Get Started in Art Licensing,

Surface Designs or Patterns

Spoonflower is probably the most popular site to at least start selling your surface designs. Your digital patterns are printed on fabric, wallpaper and gift wrap.

PatternBank is somewhat similar to Spoonflower, only you get a 55-60% commission on sales from that site. They target fashion designers, so the market seems to be a bit different, and you'll have to decide which one works better for you.

Wholesale Trade Shows

At a wholesale show, exhibitors bring one sample of each item they wholesale, unlike a public craft fair where multiples of each item are brought. Buyers will place orders and the artist will produce the order after the show and ship it to the store, usually within 4-6 weeks. In this way, artists are not required to keep a large inventory of their work on hand or purchase raw materials far in advance of the show.

Artists need to bring order forms and catalogs or brochures with images of their work. The goal of selling your work at wholesale is to sell in small quantities and get re-orders from store buyers.

American Made Show -
https://americanmadeshow.com/

ASD Market Week -
http://www.asdonline.com/

American Craft Makers Expo (ACRE) -
www.acrephiladelphia.com/
www.acrelasvegas.com/

Craft Shows & Local Markets

Go out and visit as many different shows as possible. Visit ALL the local ones, no matter how small, plus as many farther-away ones as financially possible. Eventually you can use the **Art Fair Source Book** (https://artfairsourcebook.com/) to find the best shows. Don't bother when starting out, you won't get into them anyway.

Visiting a show, look at everything: the quality of the art, the number of shoppers, how many of them seem to be buying, how happy or busy the artists seem to be. Talk to the artists, especially the ones who are showing work similar to yours. Go on the last day of a multi-day show, so the artists know how well they did. "I'm thinking about doing this show next year, how was it for you?" is a good question to ask. Most artists are happy to share info. It's how they started too.

Take notes on displays, tents, and products.

Read everything available about doing shows. Get all the necessary equipment – tent, display system, boxes for your work. Start with small local shows (make your beginner mistakes there) and work your way up into the better shows.

Finding the shows where your work sells is trial-and-error. Keep careful track of all of your show-related expenses. You might have a few more sales at an "away" show but if the hotel costs eat it all then it's not worthwhile. It takes a few years to find the gems.

MY EXPERIENCE WITH CRAFT SHOWS . . .

Craft Shows are not for the faint-of-heart. I have years of experience in hauling merchandise, setting up tents and displays and dealing with unexpected weather emergencies. It can be fun and lucrative, or it can be a sadly disappointing venture. If you choose to go this route, the number one piece of advice is do your homework and be realistic. Just because the organizers of the show report "thousands" of attendees that doesn't mean you are going to have sales. In fact, there have been many situations that I have sold more at a small, intimate home show with 15 guests than I have at craft show with a thousand attendees.

Consignment

Selling on consignment can be a scary proposition for creatives. You may have a number of people asking you to put your items in their shop, but before you do, take a look at the important do's and don'ts.

DON'T just put your goods into any shop. New shops that are looking for inventory are often where the worst things happen. It's only safe if you know and TRUST the shop owner.

DON'T go for shops that will accept anything. The best ones are juried!

DO look for shops that sell your niche.

DO look for shops that have beautiful and creative setups.

DO make sure to have a signed agreement that outlines payment, breakage or theft.

Home or Business Shows

Hold invitation-only shows at homes, salons or offices. Some of your best customers will enjoy hosting events like this for a variety of reasons. You could also join forces with a non-profit to make this a fundraising event and create a win-win situation for everyone involved. Make sure you and your host combine forces to publicize the event via press and social media to get the most out of your time and efforts.

Pop-Up Shops

Pop-up shops are a great way to promote your work and test out new products. Apply to one of these temporary retail projects and get yourself out there!

Etsy's Seller Handbook is the Bible for selling on Etsy. Visit the site at: www.etsy.com/seller-handbook/. Here's a look at what you'll find.

Photography - How-to's and best practices for representing your brand and products.

Shipping - Tips and tricks to save you money and time when fulfilling your orders.

Branding and marketing - Developing and promoting your brand to shoppers and the press, plus how to excel in customer service.

Legal - Demystifying intellectual property law, legal structures for your business and more.

Pricing, taxes and finance - Practical information to take the stress out of pricing your items, bookkeeping and taxes.

Productivity - Strategies for working smarter, not harder, including tips on hiring and leadership.

Getting found - The ins and outs of SEO and connecting with buyers on Etsy and beyond.

Growth strategies - Advice on expanding your business with new products, Etsy Wholesale or manufacturing partnerships.

My Etsy Story . . . I've been an Etsy seller since 2009 and have enjoyed great success over the years. If you're interested in learning more about setting up a successful Etsy shop, stay tuned for upcoming classes and e-books through the Grow A Creative Biz website.

Example of my Etsy shop - Azante Designs

Sell Registry Community Blogs Mobile Gift Cards	Hi, Love to Create. Your Shop: AzanteDesigns Your Account Help

Etsy   Search for items and shops   Search   Cart

Shop
Shop Dashboard

Listings
Add New Item
Listings Manager
Earn Free Listings
Sections
Shipping Profiles

Orders

Shop Stats for Oct 2012 - Dec 2012

Stats for [Specific Dates ▾] From: 10/01/2012 To: 12/31/2012 Apply

Overview   Map

Views ?	Favorites ?	Orders	Revenue ?
27,706	**1,115**	**528**	**$ 14,212.70** USD
7,410 shop views 20,296 listing views	159 shop favorites 956 listing favorites	View Orders for 2012	

MAKING IT ALL WORK

BUSINESS STRUCTURE
LEGAL ISSUES
INSURANCE
HUMAN RESOURCES

"ENTREPRENUERSHIP IS LIVING A FEW YEARS
of your life like most people won't
so you can spend the rest of your life like most people can't."

Different Types of Businesses, Different Considerations

Whether you are just opening your doors or have been in business for many years, the structure of your business may impact your liability and has tax ramifications. You can organize your business in a variety of ways. Each has advantages that can make your life easier as a business owner.

The most common types of business organizations are sole proprietorships and corporations. The Limited Liability Company, or LLC, is rapidly becoming popular and offers many advantages to new entrepreneurs.

Sole Proprietorship

- One person operating a business as an individual
- The most common type of business organization
- Easy to set up and maintain. A business permit is available at the county or city clerk's office where the business is located.
- Little government regulation and reporting
- Profits are taxed as income to the owner personally at a rate that is usually lower than corporate tax rates
- Complete control of the business, but the owner is also personally responsible for all debts & liabilities

Limited Liability Company "LLC"

- LLCs are rapidly becoming a popular form of business because they are easy to establish and maintain
- An LLC may provide many of the tax benefits of sole proprietorship or partnership. They also shield personal assets from business debts and liabilities. LLC owners risk only their investment.
- As a separate entity, an LLC can acquire assets, incur liabilities and conduct business.
- A single-member LLC is similar to a sole proprietorship with the added benefit protecting limited liability of personal assets.
- A Limited Liability Partnership (LLP) is similar to the LLC with the exception that it is aimed at professional organizations.

"C" Corporation and Non-Profit 501(3)(c)

- A legal entity comprised of persons who have received a charter that legally recognizes the corporation as a separate entity having its own rights, privileges and liabilities, apart from those of the individuals forming the corporation.
- Non-profit entities are looked at as a tax identification status. They need board of directors and formal

Legal Issues for a Creative Biz

Purchase Agreement

If you are purchasing a business, there are forms that you can use that provide a checklist. The most common is the real estate form for the purchase of commercial property. Use it even if no real estate is involved since the rest of the commercial venture is covered in the form.

Sales Contracts

This can be nothing more than an invoice to a formal document signed by seller and purchaser. In one, the invoice, there are implied promises that the property sold is fit for the purpose for which it is intended (covered under the Uniform Commercial Code, which is part of state statutes). In the other, the fine print may be more or less restrictive by providing warranties or limits of liability.

Delinquent Accounts

Otherwise known to your accountant as 'accounts receivable'. Accountants flag these as a danger point. If your account receivables are too high, it means that you have some bad accounts that are not paying. You should either get them to pay or drop them immediately. You cannot work for nothing and survive.

Employment Agreements

When you hire employees, the state requires you to publish a number of notices. Along with those notices, write a manual of prohibited practices that you do not like and enforce it. Make no exceptions. It will be a protection against unemployment compensation and other claims. Establishing an employee handbook will define legal and human resource issues as well.

Liability

Buy insurance. Work with an agent that you trust. It is a buyer's market, so do not let anyone put you down. Shop around. Worker's compensation insurance is mandatory if you have employees. So is unemployment compensation insurance. Other non-mandatory insurance is premises liability insurance that covers someone who slips and falls in your place. Fire insurance with extended coverage will cover your property loss as well as business interruption. If you sell a product, you should have product liability insurance. Talk to your agent and ask him / her to cover you for what you do.

Verbal Agreements

These are often said 'not to be worth the paper they are written on'. They are an invite to a lawsuit since a judge or jury must decide who is telling the truth. Avoid them and do not rely on a handshake. Put it in writing.

Just like other kinds of property, intellectual property needs to be protected from unauthorized use. There are four ways to protect different types of intellectual property:

1. Patents

Patents provide rights for up to 20 years for inventions. Issued by the U.S. Patent and Trademark Office (USPTO), a patent grants property rights to the inventor(s). The patent "excludes others from making, using, offering for sale, or selling" the invention in the United States or "importing" the invention into the United States. If the invention is found to be new, useful, and unobvious a patent covering the invention is issued. There are three broad categories of patents.

Inventors have the option of filing a **provisional application for patent** which provides a lower-cost for a first patent filing. A provisional application allows filing without a formal patent claim, oath or declaration, or any information disclosure (prior art) statement. It provides the means to establish an early effective filing date in a non-provisional patent application and allows the term "Patent Pending" to be applied. For more patent information – call the USPTO's General Information Services Division at 1-800-PTO-9199 or visit **www.uspto.gov/main/patents.htm.**

2. Trademarks

Trademarks protect words, names, symbols, sounds, or colors that distinguish the source of goods and services. Trademarks, unlike patents, can be renewed forever as long as they are being used in business. The roar of the MGM lion, the pink of the Owens-Corning Pink Panther and the shape of a Coca-Cola bottle are familiar trademarks. For specific trademark questions or for more information about trademarks in general, contact the Trademark Assistance Center at 1-800-786-9199 or visit **www.uspto.gov/main/trademarks.htm.**

3. Copyrights

Copyrights protect works of authorship, such as writings, music, and works of art that have been tangibly expressed. This protection is available to both published and unpublished works. The Copyright Office registers copyrights, which last the life of the author plus 70 years. *Gone With The Wind* (the book and the film), Beatles recordings, and video games are all works that are copyrighted. For questions or more information visit **www.copyright.gov.**

People Count!

"Creativepreneurs must not underestimate their own value to motivate themselves and those around them."

Surround yourself with positive people who believe in your vision. Advisors, partners, volunteers and employees are an asset to your business. You can not function without them. They are one of your great competitive strengths. That includes yourself and any family members involved. Remember, you can't grow a business alone in a vacuum. You need to build a team to help you succeed.

Things to Consider:

- Always be looking - Find good people before you actually need them.
- Staffing - Look at all the options before hiring. Can the position be filled with a volunteer, a free-lancer or a virtual assistant?
- Scheduling - Make sure you're staffed for busy periods.
- Training & Mentoring - Make sure you have a plan in place.
- Communication - Have meetings, online conferences or regular calls to keep everyone on the same page.
- Compensation - Will they be hourly or salaried? Do you have benefits?
- Motivation - Have a plan in place.
- Establish an employee handbook
- Performance - How will you review each persons performance?

Human resource management is a major stumbling block for creativepreneurs. The assumption that, "I can manage people because I have been around," is dangerous. You may find it valuable to hire an advisor to set up your personnel systems and help in hiring and training. While the cost may seem high initially, the cost of a poor hiring process can be catastrophic.

Businesses stand or fall on the strength of their personnel. Good employees and contractors can make a marginal deal go well; poor ones can destroy the best business.

"To motivate your team, focus on forward progress. Then get out of the way and let them achieve greatness."

Basic equation:

Ability x Motivation = Performance

Goals ⟹ Incentive to obtain goal

Expectation encourages us to participate

How to motivate:

Programs designed to offer an incentive to return for additional business are good for loyal customers but also staff and an outside team.

Incentive Programs:

A planned activity designed to motivate people to achieve an organization's objectives.

Examples of objectives:

- Delivering your Value Proposition
- Carrying out your Vision & Mission
- Supporting community causes
- Understanding what it takes to be profitable

Incentive program:

Must have a clear goal – emotional value and reachable. Don't forget to include your outside enterprise team for recognition, training and engagement.

The blueprint for executing the program:

- Clear objective
- Establish strategy
- Measure performance
- Prepare budget
- Select right incentive rewards
- Give platform for celebration

Merchandise and travel outperformed cash by 50% as a motivator according to the Incentive Federation. Cash was considered unemotional, an ongoing entitlement – not shared by the rest of the family.

Personal letters to family of staff, volunteers and advisors goes a long way in gaining support of your business and it's mission.

"Leadership is the ability to get extraordinary achievement from ordinary people"

-Brian Tracy

Do You Need Insurance For Your Business?

Small employers have to deal with a large array of insurance needs such as auto insurance, worker's compensation insurance, property and casualty insurance, liability insurance, flood insurance, health insurance, and life insurance. Some types of coverage are required by law while others simply make good business sense.

If you operate a full or part-time business you will need both property and liability insurance. To determine your business insurance needs, you should begin with an analysis of your property and your risks. Your property is the building and equipment you own. Your risks are the financial responsibilities you have for the people and property within your business.

Purchasing insurance is like purchasing any other product or service. Insurance companies vary substantially both in the price of their policies and the level of service to consumers. The more you know the better prepared you are to ask the right questions and make the right choices.

"Great vision without great people is irrelevant."

– Jim Collins

Insuring the Business

Many insurance companies have developed package policies for small business owners that combine property and liability coverage into what is commonly called a business owner's policy (BOP). A BOP allows you to obtain broad coverage with affordable premiums. The BOP is designed to meet the insurance needs of small offices, stores, apartment houses, certain types of small services, and processing businesses.

Many insurance agents concentrate on homeowners and auto insurance. Be sure to contact an agent with experience in commercial insurance.

Factors to consider when purchasing insurance:

- Probability of loss
- Resources available to meet the loss
- Size of potential loss

You may also want to review the document:

Consumer's Guide to Insurance for Small Business Owners

http://oci.wi.gov/pub_list/pi-085.pdf

Types of coverage commonly considered for small business owners:

Fire and General Property Insurance

- Covering fire losses, vandalism, hail, and wind damage.

Plate-Glass Insurance

- Covering window damage.

Consequential-Loss Insurance

- Covering loss of earnings or extra expenses when business is suspended due to a fire or other catastrophe.

Burglary Insurance

- Covering forced entry and theft of merchandise and cash.

Fidelity Bonding

- Covering theft by an employee

Fraud Insurance

- Covering counterfeit money, bad checks, and larceny as well as stolen credit cards.

Public Liability Insurance

- Covering injury to the public such as customers or pedestrians falling on the property.

Product Liability Insurance

- Covering injury to customers arising from the use of goods purchased through the business.

Worker's Compensation Insurance

- Covering injury to employees at work.

Life Insurance

- Covering the life of the owner(s) or key employee(s).

Business Interruption Insurance
Malpractice Insurance

- Covering owner against claims from customers who suffer damages as a result of services performed.

Errors and Omission Insurance

- Covering the business against claims from customers who suffer injuries or loss because of errors made or things that should have been done but were not.

Most people do not think twice about the price of insuring their vehicles. Yet most business owners neglect an insurance strategy that includes insuring their most important assets – themselves and their business.

Owning your own space is a separate investment with it's own cash outlay. Leases, however, are a fixed expense.

"Understand what you are signing with any lease, purchase or rental agreement."

Flat Lease

- One set cost

Triple Net Lease

- Square footage
- Property taxes
- CAM cost (common area maintenance - insurance, utilities, maintenance)

Heads up to look for:

- Be aware while you are sub-leasing
- Percentage of sales will cut into profit
- Automatic increases
- Move-in dates - Negotiate if you need more time before you actually launch
- Liability coverage for you and your landlord - who pays?
- Lawn care and snow removal
- Dumpster location
- Freight delivery and pick-up
- Safety and security issues
- Dealing with real estate broker versus owner

- Signage requirements/local regulations
- Accessibility / parking
- Repairs - whose responsibility?
- Hours of operation

Home Based Business

- Understand all the tax savings and regulations
- Ask your tax accountant

Negotiate...Negotiate...Negotiate!

Your lease is one of your biggest fixed expenses!

Important Tip:

Rent = The cost of space and advertising

High traffic area means less advertising is needed. A more remote location requires more advertising to drive clients.

Location, Location, Location

If you've ever heard this old adage about real estate it's even more important when it comes to a business location. Being in the right location can make or break your business.

Before you start shopping for business space, you need to have a clear picture of what you must have, what you'd like to have, what you absolutely won't tolerate and how much you're able to pay. Consider who your customers are and how important their proximity to your location is. For a retailer and some service providers, this is critical; for other types of businesses, it might not be as important. Are competing companies located nearby? Sometimes that's good, such as in industries where comparison shopping is popular.

Find out if any ordinances or zoning restrictions could affect your business in any way. Many older buildings don't have the necessary infrastructure to support the high-tech needs of contemporary operations.

Rent composes the major portion of your ongoing facilities expense, but consider extras such as utilities--they're included in some leases but not in others.

Scout out several locations. Are you a destination business or do you need other common businesses surrounding you? Look at your location as part of your branding and overall image. Part of your perceived value depends on where you are located.

Rate each location by using a grading system

Rating 1-10

______ Demographics of customer / proximity to your market

______ Competition

______ Labor supply

______ Physical features of the building (renovations)

______ Zoning (signage as well)

______ Business street and address

______ Taxes

______ Dept. of Transportation traffic count and plans

Rating 1-10

______ Image of local area

______ Business climate - success rate

______ Proximity to supplies

______ Parking availability

______ Accessibility

______ Types of business in area

______ Future value of area

______ Expansion capabilities

______ Leases

______ **TOTAL**

ALL ABOUT THE $$$

FINANCIALS
THE ART OF PRICING

"BUILD YOUR OWN DREAMS
OR SOMEONE ELSE WILL GET YOU
TO BUILD THEIRS."

-Farrah Gray

Financial statements are the means of communicating business information. They help you to evaluate your business past, present and future. Think of your financial statement as the telling of your business story over the past month or year.

NOTE . . . Accounting doesn't have to be an exact science. Estimates and assumptions are often used to put your plans together. Don't get stumped by trying to provide exact numbers when getting started. Obviously, exact numbers are necessary for reporting and taxes, but in planning, estimates are perfectly fine.

- **Be aware that a tax accountant should be utilized.**
- **Solid, honest bookkeeping systems are important.**
- **Realize the importance of timely, estimated tax payments in your business.**

The following should be part of your business mindset.

- Reading and analyzing financial statements.
- Determining the financial strengths and weaknesses of the firm.
- Planning and taking necessary corrective action.
- Analyzing the components of the balance sheet and profit and loss statements.

- Importance of reviewing your pricing strategy.
- Determining the cash flow needs of the firm.
- Proper balance of investments in assets such as a building, fixtures, and other equipment.
- Sound management of both short-term and long-term debts.
- Sound credit terms and practices for selling on credit.
- A reasonable appraisal of whether or not you are realizing an adequate rate of return on your investment, based on the amount invested in your business and the time you devote to it.

"Having a business mindset as a creativepreneur is one of the most important things you can do to ensure success and sustainability."

Assets:

Assets are balance sheet entries **that show what your business owns**. Assets can be categorized as current, fixed, intangible, or other. These categories are based on the availability of items, that is, the length of time it takes to convert them to cash.

- Current assets are assets that in the normal course of business are expected to be converted into cash within twelve months. It includes cash on hand, accounts receivable and inventory.
- Fixed assets are those items that usually cannot be changed into cash within twelve months. They are items that the business acquired for long-term use. Fixed assets include land, buildings, machinery, equipment, and company vehicles.
- Intangible assets are goodwill – value that a business gains from its customers; franchise fees paid; patents and copyrights.
- Other assets are miscellaneous items of value – stocks, bonds, in other companies; cash value of life insurance policies.

Liabilities:

Liabilities are anything that the business owes. Liabilities might include loans, credit notes, income taxes, and mortgages.

- Current liabilities are obligations the business owes to some individual or firm that will be paid by a current asset within twelve months. "Accounts Payable" is the most common type of current liability.
- Also included are withholding and social security taxes payable and that part of a long term debt that is payable within one year.
- Long term liabilities are those debts that are due after twelve months – mortgages and long term loans.
- Net worth is the owned portion of the business. It is the owner's investment in a single proprietorship, the partners' investment in a partnership or an individual's investment in corporate stocks.

A profit and loss statement is a record of the activities of a business during a period of time. Example: month – quarter – year

Components of a profit and loss statement:

- **Total sales** include both cash and credit sales. It does not include sales tax collected or the sales figures for products returned.
- **The Cost of Goods Sold (COGS)** is the amount that it costs you to buy or produce the goods that you sold. If you are a manufacturer, you will also inventory raw materials and products in process and include this information. The cost of goods sold is calculated by:
    - Taking a beginning inventory
    - Adding materials or products purchased during the accounting period
    - Subtracting inventory remaining at the end of the accounting period

Gross margin is the amount of profit made from sales before operating expenses are deducted. Gross margin is calculated by subtracting the cost of goods sold from the total sales.

- **Expenses** include all costs involved in running the business.

- **Selling expenses** are those expenses for activities performed to increase the sales volume.

    They include:

    - Salaries
    - Travel expenses for salespeople
    - Delivery expenses
    - Advertising

Operating expenses are those expenses made to operate and administer the business.

    They include:

    - Office expenses
    - Salaries
    - Accounting expenses
    - Telephone expenses
    - General insurance
    - Rent and leases
    - Marketing
    - Website & internet
    - Bank & processing fees

Net profit is your profit or loss at the end of the accounting period. This does not include taxes you must pay on the business.

Controlling Operating Costs

One very important thing to establish in your business mindset is Operations. Take the time to set up a system to track time, paperwork, documents and contracts. This will save you dollars on your expenses thus protecting your business assets.

ITEMS TO REVIEW:

Transportation Costs

- Control your "express" deliveries and shipments
- Watch your freight and delivery costs
- Do not pay for backorder shipping costs
- Negotiate shipping costs
- Watch where your supplies come from
- Indicate on your purchase orders how to ship
- Try to avoid C.O.D. charges

Telephone Costs

- Watch for hidden costs in phone plans
- Internet access

Administration

Organize files:

- Sales
- Accounts payable
- Expense contracts
- Year-end
- Receivables

- Correspondence
- Protecting assets

Audit and Review

- Energy bills
- Repair and maintenance costs
- Transportation and delivery costs

Purchase Orders

- Construct your own with your terms.
- Do not use supply store or vendor/supplier copies.

Inventory Control

- Understand the principle of inventory turns, old stock and the cost of storage. Consider Real Time ordering.

Insurance

- Read between the lines

Collecting your money

- You need cash flow

Safety

- Establish a safety checklist

Office and building security

- Alarm systems, key policies

Check control / fraud

- Procedures and lock-up are important

Internal theft

- Don't be naive; preventive

Expenses control

- Everything costs money!

Productivity control

- Biggest factor is time card management

External theft

- Evaluate all scenarios

Internet and computer security

- Reevaluate every year

Copyright, patents, intellectual property

- See legal chapter

Establish an employee handbook

- You will look at it differently as an employer versus an employee

Secure storage

- Key financial and legal documents
- Keys – vehicles, safes, buildings, drawers

- Passwords
- Company minutes and records
- Computer backup disks
- Shredders
- Customer list
- Tools
- Office supplies

Other computer needs

- Wireless
- Firewalls

Equipment

- Phones
- Copier
- Printers
- Computers
- Postal machines
- Faxes

Protecting against fraud

- Check supply
- Online protection
- Procedures and controls
- Limit people with authorizations

Collections

- Invoices – make sure you are on top of sending out billing
- Understand the Fair-Debt collection practices
- Know when to go to collections, small claims or an attorney

How do you price your products or services as a creative entrepreneur?

Pricing is probably one of the most challenging things facing creativepreneurs. Pricing of your products or services requires careful consideration of industry or competitive pricing, market research, cost of goods sold and the subjective factor of "What the Market will Bear". Pricing needs to cover all of the costs of making your product or providing your service, not just your time. Too often equipment, supplies, allocation of general costs, benefits, taxes, training and marketing are overlooked.

Believe in Your Value

Creatives may think that a low price will generate more sales. The opposite is really true. When you charge too little or apply discounts continually, customers perceive that as a lack of experience or skill. They also may perceive that you're not offering a quality product or service.

Secondly, low prices attract customers or clients that make decisions based on price instead of quality. These are the hardest customers to please and the least loyal. If you don't value yourself and your talents, how can anyone else? Also keep in mind with creative products or services, it's about perceived value - which is very different to the actual cost value of your products. Branding, marketing, photography, the customer experience, and packaging all influence customers about what your products are worth, beyond the price of the materials/supplies.

Don't Underestimate the True Costs

Start by determining the Cost of Goods Sold (COGS). These are the direct costs attributable to the production of the goods sold in a company. It's important to keep track of all the materials you use in creating your product or service. Also note the cost of delivering the service or product which includes packaging and postage. This will give you a good idea of the cost of materials used for each product.

Don't Forget Hidden Costs & Labor

Many times, entrepreneurs forget some of the hidden costs that can add up and reduce your bottom line profit.

- **Labor** - factor in costs for your own labor as well as any outsourcing you use to create your product or service.
- **Equipment** - factor in depreciation on any larger pieces of equipment. Also include purchase and rental of equipment.
- **Operating Expenses** - your overhead including all office expenses, supplies, insurance (business & health),
- **Sales & Marketing Expenses** - even if you are performing these items yourself, don't forget to include your time as a labor cost.

- **Administrative Expenses** - this can be your time, an employee or someone you outsource.
- **Packaging & Shipping Expenses** - Take into account all the items needed to package and ship your product from the tissue paper to the box to the mailing envelope, postage and time needed to properly package each item.

Pricing needs to be sustainable and designed to make a profit

Creativepreneurs often don't plan for profit in their business when they set their prices. Remember, not everyone may be able to afford handcrafted art, but that's not your fault. If this reality is upsetting, consider offering a few items with lower production costs.

Cost of Goods Sold + Operating Expenses = Break Even Point

Reality Check

If the value and quality of your product is not apparent, which is often the case, you will never achieve your best price.

Price Sensitivities

Elasticity refers to the degree that a change inprice affects the demand. You must understand to take advantage and recognize opportunities to raise or lower prices. Your brand plays a major role in determining price.

A story to share . . .

We recently met an artist who makes high-end stained glass art and does installations in multi-million dollar homes. She loves art and sharing her talent so in addition to her high end art pieces, she offers a few small glass brooches for $25. She also uses these as a value-added item. When someone purchases a large piece, she offers them one of the brooches as a special thank you gift.

She shared with us that on several occasions children have come into her booth admiring her beautiful, sun-kissed pieces of glass art and handed her 25¢ for the glass brooch which is marked at 25 (dollars, that is). After a short conversation about art and her creative journey she honors them by presenting them with the glass art brooch which she beautifully packages in a decorative bag.

The moral of the story is this . . . price for profit, but never forget as an artisan you have special talents and it's alright now and then to share your gift!

"To charge more than your competition, you have to make yourself stand apart to justify the difference."

GROWING YOUR CREATIVE BUSINESS

VENTURING & GROWTH
BUYING & SELLING A BUSINESS
INVESTORS

"BUILD YOUR OWN DREAMS
OR SOMEONE ELSE WILL GET YOU
TO BUILD THEIRS."
-Farrah Gray

Growth and Expansion

Broadening the Pond

When growing your business you must commit the substantial time, energy and necessary capital.

When deciding on whether to grow you should ask yourself:

- What is my time commitment to my family?
- What type of long-term lifestyle do I require or want?
- Will I continue to have a vision of innovation and change?
- Do I have the passion?

Venturing Requires:

- Going beyond your comfort zones
- Raising the bar in goal-setting
- Ongoing product and service innovation
- Strong mentoring techniques
- A "feel" (intuitive) for decision making
- Investment in personal assets
- Managing change
- Trend responding

Succession or Exit Strategy

- Passing on to family members
- Selling portion or all of the business
- Employee stock option (ESOP)
- Liquidation

Venturing encourages and fosters new ideas within your company. It does involve risk so you must be prepared to manage and control them.

"For me, the most fun is change or growth. There are definitely elements of both that I like. Launching a business is kind of like a motorboat: You can go very quickly and turn fast."

- Tony Hsieh, CEO of Zappos.com

Surviving Growth: Expansion Traps

Facts:

- Growth is not necessarily the same as success
- Profits are essential
- You can remain small and still compete

Traps:

- Forgetting the customer
- Failing to diversify the market
- Automating too soon
- Assuming too much debt
- Failing to take good advice
- Refusing to get help
- Loss of creativity
- Forgetting your business plan
- Ignoring the numbers
- Lack of controls
- Building a bureaucracy: Too much paperwork
- Failing to change
- Taking the wrong risks
- Inadequate insurance
- Leaving employees out
- Ignoring employee talent
- Spending excessively
- Depending on consultants
- Failing to plan taxes
- Volume trap
- Expanding executive layers
- Geography traps

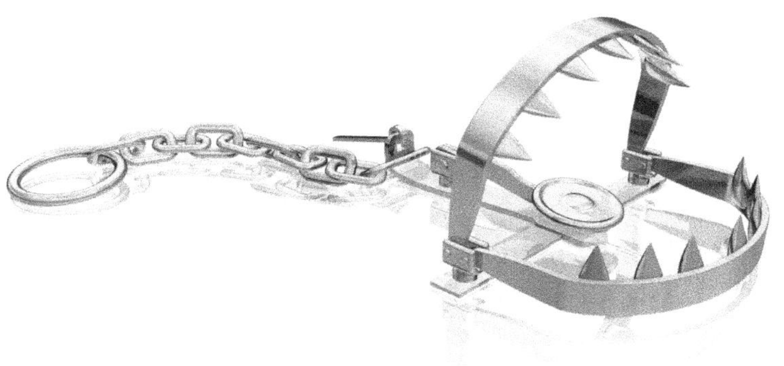

"Creative innovators are moving into new frontiers. The evolutionary entrepreneur will bring creativity, innovation, and social enterprising to their journey. To evolve we may need to take detours, but always be evolving ."

- Mark Burwell

How Much is that Business in the Window?

A dollar figure can be placed on a business's physical assets, but the true value is what the buyer will actually pay for it.

In a nutshell, it comes down to the buyer's reason to buy:

- Where it is for financial gain
- A competitor for strategic positioning
- An entrepreneur who has a vision to carry on the mission or grow into a new one

Goodwill intangible assets do not play an important part. The key factors are:

- Are they branded and have a certain image
- Employees' goodwill, skills and training
- Industry analysis and competition
- Depth of key mentors and leaders
- Past market penetration

Capacity for future profit is what is important to a buyer. What is the earnings potential?

Buying an already progressive, positive growth business is worth more than a business that has been told to downsize to make the balance sheet look good, has underlying expenses and employee challenges. These are red flags that the business does not have income potential in the future.

Planning and Preparation When Buying and Selling

- See a tax accountant on tax issues
- Settle any legal/employee/labor issues ahead of time
- Do not give up on running your current operation
- Evaluate lease arrangement
- Look at testimonials and references
- Do not over evaluate your business
- Do not drag on a sale
- Settle any family issues on business or personnel nature
- Keep confidential – make sure confidentiality agreements are signed
- Negotiate and be flexible by understanding the importance of the succession. It is a process not an event.
- Understand the financial bank loan situation. You may have to be creative on your financing as buyers and sellers.

"Success is not the key to happiness. Happiness is the key to success. If you love what you are doing, you will be successful."

- Albert Schweitzer

Creative entrepreneurs have many avenues for funding in today's business playing field, including:

- Traditional financial lenders
- Local economic development funds
- Crowd funding
- Angel investors

Below are points to improve communication with your investors:

- Know exactly what you want to say.
- Rehearse your presentation several times.
- Have your materials ready.
- Talk the investors language.
- Make your presentation simple and to the point.
- Speak clearly. Be confident and enthusiastic.
- Use visual aids.
- Listen to other opinions and encourage interaction from your audience.
- Anticipate questions your audience may bring up and be prepared with an answer or be willing to find the answer.
- Close on a positive note, and make sure everyone understands what has been decided. Know what the next step will be.

- Do not get upset when people disagree with you.
- Do not allow arguments.
- Do not let the meeting bog down.

If for some reason the investor turns down your loan request, it is important to view this not as a flaw in your character or as a spot on your company's reputation, but as an opportunity to turn this rejection into something productive.

Find out why and obtain specific answers as to the problem with your business, the application or your style. Find out if there is a problem with the bank. Possibly the bank or investors are not making loans at this time and you were simply caught in an economic cycle. If possible, get a written reply.

If they indicate that you have a poor credit rating, check the bank's source of a credit report. Perhaps some of this information is incorrect and you can challenge it or at least change it before you submit a loan proposal elsewhere. Ask the investor for suggestions on how to improve your loan application and if at all possible, get a referral. Perhaps they know of another financial resource that would be more receptive to your proposal.

The 5 C's of Credit (Information Necessary to Underwrite a Loan)

COLLATERAL - Business plan and loan request

- Amount requested
- Sources and uses of funds
- Term of loan
- Purpose of loan
    - Purchase agreement if acquisition loan
    - Construction cost breakdown if construction loan
- Leases
- Collateral available description (i.e. appraisal, environment)
- Source of repayment
- Expected benefits

CONDITIONS - Description of borrowing entity)

- Company background
- Ownership structure (include formation documentation)
- Products and services
- Markets and customers
- Competition
- Unique characteristics

CAPACITY AND CAPITAL - Financial balance sheets and income statement

Business:

- Income and expense statements (include 3 years of historical operations)
- Balance sheets
- Accounts receivable aging report
- Accounts payable aging report
- Fixed asset listing
- Loan/borrowing list

Personal financial statements of owners:

- Three years of tax returns
- Balance sheet
- Portfolio summary for real estate

CHARACTER - Ownership biographical sketch)

- Owners resume
- Management experience or management contract
- Key employees
- Professional advisers (Example: Accountant, attorney, architect, general contractor)

RESOURCES

SOCIAL MEDIA SIZES
CREATIVEPRENEUR TOOLKIT
DONATION FORM

"YOU MUST DO THE THING YOU
THINK YOU CANNOT DO."

-Eleanor Roosevelt

2018 Social Media Image Sizes Cheat Sheet

FACEBOOK

Cover image: 828 x 315

Profile image: 180 x 180

Shared image: 1200 x 900

Shared link preview image: 1200 x 628

TWITTER

Header image: 1500 x 500

Profile image: 400 x 400

Timeline image: 506 x 253

GOOGLE+

Profile image: 250 x 250

Cover image: 1080 x 608

Shared image: 506 pixels wide

Shared video: 506 x 284

Shared link image thumbnail: 150 x 150

INSTAGRAM

Profile image: 110 x 110

Image thumbnail: 161 x 161

Shared images: 1080 x 1080

Shared videos: 1080 pixels wide

PINTEREST

Profile image: 180 x 180

Board cover image: 214 x 100

Pin preview: 238 pixels wide

LINKEDIN

Banner image: 1850 x 200

Profile image: 400 x 400

Cover image: 1536 x 768

Shared image: 350 pixels wide

Shared link preview: 180 x 110

Logo image: 400 x 400

YOUTUBE

Channel cover images: Varies by viewing platform

Channel icon: 800 x 800

Video thumbnail: 1280 x 720

TUMBLR

Profile image: 128 x 128

Image post: 500 x 750 | 1280 x 1920 maximum

All dimensions are in pixels, width x height.

"The Ultimate Creativepreneur Toolkit"

Essential Tools and Resources (many free!) to Help You Build Your Creative Biz

(for the full Toolkit featuring hundreds of resources, visit our site at www.growacreativebiz.com)

DESIGN SOFTWARE

- **Canva** - www.canva.com - Easy-to-use design tool for social media posts as well as brochures, business cards, and a variety of marketing materials. Free - some paid upgrades.
- **Photo Collage** - www.photocollage.com - Create collages, add text and then easily save them for Facebook, Twitter and Google+ Cover Photos. Free.

FONTS/TYPOGRAPHY

- **Dafont** - www.dafont.com - Lots of fonts (not all free for commercial use}
- **Font Squirrel** - www.fontsquirrel.com - Free fonts

STOCK PHOTOS, BACKROUNDS, ICONS

- **Can Stock Photos** - https://canstockphoto.com
- **Unsplash** - https://unsplash.com
- **Pixabay** - https://pixabay.com
- **Gratisography** - https://www.gratisography.com
- **Life of Pix** - http://www.lifeofpix.com
- **FreePik** - http://www.freepik.com
- **StockSnap** - https://stocksnap.io

MOCKUPS, DESIGN ELEMENTS, TEMPLATES, FONT BUNDLES, ETC

- **Creative Market** - www.creativemarket.com - Sign up to emails for weekly freebies
- **Design Cuts** -www.designcuts.com - discounted design bundles (free and paid)
- **PSD Covers** - www.PSDcovers.com - Photoshop product mockups

COLOR PALETTE DESIGN

- **Coolors Color Scheme Generator** - www.coolors.co - Generate color schemes to help you create your Brand Style Guide.
- **Adobe Color CC**- https://color.adobe.com/create/image/- Create a palette from an image

PHOTO-EDITING SOFTWARE

- **PicMonkey** – www.picmonkey.com - Free photo editing software with additional features for paid subscribers. A fantastic tool for editing or designing images for your social media posts.
- **Gimp** - www.gimp.org - GIMP is likely the most popular free photo editing program. It's full of professional features and provides a very friendly and flexible interface. GIMP works with Windows, Linux, and Mac operating systems.

EMAIL TOOLS

- **Mailchimp** - www.mailchimp.com - Free for up to 2000 subscribers
- **Mailerlite** - www.mailerlite.com - Free for up to 1000 subscribers
- **HelloBar** - www.hellobar.com - Free tool used to collect more subscribers on your website

SOCIAL MEDIA AUTOMATION TOOLS

- **Buffer** - https://buffer.com - Schedule FB, Twitter, Pinterest, G+, LinkedIn & Instagram. Free plan available (10 posts scheduled at a time). .
- **Hootsuite** - https://hootsuite.com - Schedule FB, Twitter, G+, LinkedIn, Wordpress, Instagram, Youtube. Free plan available.
- **Socioboard** - www.socioboard.com - With Socioboard, you can connect all the most popular social media accounts and manage them from one central dashboard.

EVENT CREATION & SCHEDULING

- **Eventbrite** - www.eventbrite.com - is a platform that allows event organizers to plan, promote, and sell tickets to events and publish them across Facebook, Twitter and other social-networking tools directly from the site's interface.

SELLING YOUR PRODUCTS ONLINE

- **Etsy** - www.etsy.com - Sell handmade or digital goods. Store is free, pay per listing. To get started, read the Etsy Sellers Handbook. www.etsy.com/seller-handbook
- **Artfire** - www.artfire.com - Sell handmade or vintage goods and supplies
- **Shopify** - www.shopify.com - Set up an e-commerce store. 14 day free trial
- **Big Cartel** - www.bigcartel.com - Online stores for designers, musicians and creatives.
- **WooCommerce** - https://woocommerce.com - A popular WordPress ecommerce plugin.
- **Gumroad** - https://gumroad.com - Sell digital files. Starts at $10 a month
- **Amazon** – www.amazon.com - The single largest directory of online stores. Monthly fees as well as fees for each item sold. You can ship or utilize Amazon fulfillment for a fee.

GIVEAWAYS

- **Rafflecopter** - https://www.rafflecopter.com - Giveaway tools. Free version available
- **Gleam** - https://gleam.io - Giveaway tools and marketing apps. Free version available

SURVEY CREATION

- **SurveyMonkey -** www.surveymonkey.com - Free online survey software.
- **Typeform -** www.typeform.com - Create online surveys and forms.
- **Google Surveys -** www.google.com/analytics/surveys- Market research from Google.

ANALYTICS & SEO TOOLS

- **Google Analytics** - www.google.com/analytics - Enter the Google Analytics code into your website's HTML and the service will measure certain goals for you.
- **Quill Engage** - www.quillengage.com - Simple Google Analytics reporting
- **Marmalead** - https://marmalead.com - Etsy SEO & market research tools
- **Etsy Rank** - https://etsyrank.com - Tools to analyze and grow your Etsy business
- **SimilarWeb** - www.similarweb.com - SimilarWeb lets you plug in any website or mobile app, receive insights about traffic and rankings, and compare the data against competing sites.

PRODUCTIVITY TOOLS

- **Google Drive** www.google.com/drive is a personal cloud storage service from **Google** that lets users store and synchronize digital content across computers, laptops and mobile devices, including Android-powered tablet and smartphone devices.
- **Dropbox** - www.dropbox.com is a personal cloud storage service that is frequently used for file sharing and collaboration. Free, but with the Dropbox business plan, you pay $9.99 a month for 1TB of storage and auto backup to the cloud.
- **Carbonite -** www.carbonite.com - Allows a behind-the-scenes automatic backup of all the files on your computer (you can add multiple computers and devices).
- **Google Analytics** - https://analytics.google.com - A free web analytics service offered by Google that tracks and reports website traffic.
- **Evernote** www.evernote.com - Helps capture ideas, inspiration and trends. Access it on all your devices. Perfect tool for finding and storing content ideas, research and brainstorming.
- **Remember the Milk** - www.rememberthemilk.com - To-do lists and reminders

PACKAGING

- **Boxes, bags, and all shipping needs:** www.uline.com and www.valuemailers.com
- **Gift boxes, bags, ribbon, gift wrap and packaging supplies** - www.papermart.com

PRINTING

- **Business cards, Labels, Posters, Marketing Materials, Postcards:** www.gotprint.com, www.123print.com, www.vistaprint.com
- **Retractable Banners:** www.uprinting.com

COMMUNICATION TOOLS

- **Google Hangouts** - https://hangouts.google.com - A unified communications service where members to initiate and participate in text, voice or video chats; one-on-one or in a group.
- **Skype** - https://www.skype.com/en - Call or message anyone around the world.
- **MeetingBurner** - www.meetingburner.com - Host your next webinar or meeting for up to 10 people free.

CREATIVEPRENEUR RESOURCE TOOKIT

SOCIAL MEDIA RESEARCH

- **Google Alerts** - www.google.com/alerts - Monitor the web for content. Create news alerts that send you updates via email based on the keywords you select. Great way to see what your competitors are up to and to get immediate updates on topics you're following.

WEBSITE CREATION, TEMPLATES AND HOSTING

- **Squarespace** - www.squarespace.com - Packed with features and beautiful themes.
- **Weebly** - www.weebly.com - Perfect for anyone looking for something easy to use.
- **Wix** - www.wix.com - Good option for those wanting detailed control of their website.
- **Shopify** - www.shopify.com - A strong e-commerce store builder with many templates to choose from.
- **BigCommerce** - www.bigcommerce.com - A high quality ecommerce store creator, with comprehensive set of tools to help you sell.
- **WordPress** - www.wordpress.com - Create a blog, website or online store. Learning curve is higher than some of the others but it offers thousands of custom options.
- **BlueHost** - www.bluehost.com - Domains and website hosting at reasonable prices.

ONLINE ADWORD/PPC ANALYSIS

- **Google Adwords** - https://adwords.google.com - A free AdWords tool and Keyword Planner.

ACCOUNTING & BUSINESS SERVICES

- **Quick Books Self-Employed -** https://quickbooks.intuit.com/self-employed- Cloud-based service for invoicing, mileage tracking, tax reports and links to your bank accounts.
- **Fresh Books -** www.freshbooks.com - Invoice, expenses, time-tracking and reporting.

TIME MANAGEMENT/DISTRACTION PREVENTION

- **RescueTime** - www.rescuetime.com - Helps you understand your daily habits so that you can be more productive.
- **FocusBooster**_- A digital pomodoro timer.

As a creativepreneur, you will probably be approached often by people trying to solicit donations for fundraisers, giveaways, raffles, etc. It's important to set a limit on what you will give on a yearly basis so your giving doesn't get out of control.

Establish a log and budget of donation requests.

Organization ____

Contact person ____

Address ____

Phone ____

Event ____

Date ____

Items and services ____

____

Cash amount ____

When requested ____

Needs by ____

Pick-up date ____

By ____

Purpose of donation services provided: _________________________

____

TOOLBOX & TERMS

SOCIAL MEDIA GLOSSARY
BUSINESS TERMS

"SUCCESS DOESN'T ALWAYS COME FROM THE BIG ACTIONS WE TAKE . . .

but from the sum of all the small actions we repeat."

1. Create the demand!
2. Carve out a niche by lifestyles, special hobbies or interests, a problem or needs, or corporate needs
3. "Trend Respond!"
4. Find solid mentors and advisors
5. Build on a good image of yourself, marketing and business
6. Follow-up on referrals
7. Identify your business with a solid slogan
8. Be able to handle customer objections
9. Establish a focus group
10. Create events
11. Personal and business appearance is important
12. Act like a professional
13. Watch your inventories carefully, but do not hold them down so tight that you lose sales
14. Monitor cash flow
15. Negotiate with suppliers, landlords and contractors
16. Separate the "nice to do" from the "have to do"
17. Watch receivables
18. Do not skimp on service and quality by being understaffed
19. Build your customer base
20. Maintain a solid marketing campaign
21. Maintain professional, personal and employee training
22. Get employees involved in tactics for expense cuts and waste
23. Be aware of your competition but do not be afraid of it. Buy your competition's products. Do not compete on price
24. Solicit and investigate advice and complaints
25. Act...do not react
26. The more information you have the better decision you will make
27. Do an image perception study
28. Have a customer focus group
29. Understand the buying cycle
30. Hire people who want to work for more than just money
31. Recognize mistakes and problems as windows of opportunity
32. Learn to read financial statements
33. Great customer service is when you give more than they expect
34. Network, network, network! Cupid, cupid, cupid!
35. Smile and give back to the community
36. Remember the handshake and the thank you

Common Social Media Terminology

While each platform is different, there are several terms that are common across all social media platforms.

Bio: Short description of who you are. Not used on Snapchat, Facebook, or LinkedIn.

Business Page: A free feature for companies who wish to be recognized as a business on Instagram. This feature provides a contact button that allows the company to decide how their audience can get in touch with them, as well as get directions to the brick and mortar location.

Comment: A reaction or response to a user's post that shows up beneath the post.

Follow: The act of subscribing to another user's updates or adding another user as a friend or connection on the platform. When you follow a user, everything they post will show up on your feed.

Follower: Users who subscribe to your posts on social media platforms. Synonymous with Facebook friends, Snapchat friends, and LinkedIn connections.

Handle: Your username on a platform, often preceded by "@". Handles are not used on Snapchat or LinkedIn.

Hashtag (#): A word or phrase (without spaces) preceded by a hash or pound sign to identify a keyword or topic and make it easy to track and locate. Hashtags are most commonly used on Instagram and Twitter; sometimes used on Facebook; not used on Snapchat or LinkedIn.

Giveaway/Contest: A way for users to engage with your business through methods such as repost and tag a photo, tag a friend in the comments, or like a post. Giveaways are not common on Snapchat.

Like: A virtual thumbs up to show a user you liked their post. Not used on Snapchat.

Location: The place where you are posting from, or where a photo was taken. Locations are not tagged on Snapchat (unless using a geofilter). Locations on LinkedIn are mostly used for business profiles or not used at all because the platform doesn't support GPS locations.

Mention (@): The act of tagging another user by placing the @ sign before their username. Mentions are not used on Snapchat.

Newsfeed: The "homepage" of the social media platform you're looking at, and typically the first page you're directed to immediately after logging in. Newsfeeds show a stream of information on social media that your friends or people you follow have posted including links to websites, news, pictures, and videos.

Post: Content consisting of links, text, photos, or videos that users put on their profile or news feed (depending on the platform) as a way of providing updates in real time.

Profile: Personal information on a social media channel. Other users can view your content and personal information to get a better idea of who you are and what you do.

Reply: Similar to a mention, the act of responding to another user's comment or mention by preceding their username with the @ symbol. This directly notifies them that you are responding to one of their comments.

Tag: Links another user to a post or tweet by using the @ sign before their username. Users can't tag on Snapchat.

Trend: Popular topic based on how many users have posted a topic with a specific hashtag. Snapchat does not post trends.

Username: Your handle on social media accounts such as Snapchat, Instagram, and Twitter. How other users can search for you, mention you, or reply to you.

FACEBOOK GLOSSARY

Facebook is the most widely used social media platform. In order to get the most out of marketing your business on Facebook, here's the terminology that you need to know.

Business Page: A page where businesses can post updates using text, photos, and videos to keep their customers engaged and aware of what's new. A great place to promote Facebook events, new product launches, or to promote blog posts.

Chat: Communication between users.

Facebook Event: Gives the time, location, date, and details of an event a business is holding or participating in. Companies can invite their fans to the event and encourage them to share the event on their personal pages to increase visibility.

Facebook Ads Manager: An application that allows business owners to track ad performance; edit published ads, ad budgets, and schedules; receive notifications; and create new ads.

Facebook Live: Allows users to post live videos of whatever they're doing at any given moment. Facebook lives provides an interactive way for businesses to give their audience real time updates of what their company is up to.

Fans: Facebook users who have "liked" your Facebook page.

Share: Taking content from another user and posting it to your news feed for all of your followers to see.

Status Update: Any content that you post, and can include text and media. Snapchat and Instagram users don't post status updates.

Timeline: A user's feed of their posts that is found on their profile.

INSTAGRAM GLOSSARY

Instagram is the most visual platform available to social media users. Its users can post photos and short videos to their followers. It's especially effective for small businesses to show what their products look like, or show photos of customers with their products.

Caption: Short description of a photo or video.

Direct Message/DM: One-to-one messaging between users within the app. Users don't need to follow each other to use this feature.

Filter: A way for you to personalize your photos and enhance their look.

Insta/IG: Slang used when referring to the Instagram app.

Post: A picture or video uploaded by an Instagram user.

Private Profile: Profile with settings such that you can approve or reject other users' requests to follow you and see your content.

Public Profile: Profile with settings such that any user can find your profile, follow you, and see your content.

LINKEDIN GLOSSARY

LinkedIn is the social media network for professionals, giving users a profile that serves as an online resume. On LinkedIn, users can connect with work colleagues or other users interested in the same industry.

Company Page: Where your business can post an overview of its business and engage in discussions on group pages. Users can follow your company to receive updates on their news feeds. You can also post links to the pages of affiliated businesses.

Connection: A user to whom you are connected on LinkedIn.

Degrees: Shows how you are connected to another user. Think of it like "x degrees of separation."

Groups: Groups can be created by one person or a company, and allow users to interact with each other about a specific topic or industry.

Invitation: Invite to ask someone to join your network or have you join theirs.

Network: Includes your connections, as well as the connections of your connections

SNAPCHAT GLOSSARY

Snapchat, as a newer social media platform, is rapidly growing in popularity, especially among business owners. If you're looking to use Snapchat for your business, it's a great way to post behind from the scenes of your business and connect with your audience.

Chat: A way for two users to talk to interact within the app through text.

Friend: A connection on the app. You can see each other's stories, and send chats, cash, and snaps to each other.

Geofilter: A word, doodle, or phrase that appears on the snap when the user swipes

over a picture they've taken. Business owners can use geofilters to promote their companies in certain geographical areas.

Snap: A picture or video lasting up to 10 seconds before disappearing. Users can include a short caption by tapping the screen, prompting a keyboard to pop up.

Story: Where users can post a snap for their all of their friends to view for 24 hours before it disappears.

TWITTER GLOSSARY

Users typically use Twitter to post links, media or short messages that are up to 140 characters in length.

Direct Message/DM: One-to-one messaging between users within the app. Users must be following each other to use this feature.

Retweet (RT): When a user re-shares your message with their followers on Twitter.

Tweet: A message consisting of up to 140 characters and can include other visual media

Having a vocabulary of social media lingo will help you better communicate with other users and followers, which can boost audience engagement and increase online visibility. A social media vocabulary will also allow you to stay tuned in to what people are talking about when discussing trends in your industry, or even just the platforms in general. This, in turn, will show your audience that you are up-to-date with social technology and new marketing methods, which can increase your credibility.

"We don't have a choice of whether we DO social media. The question is how well we DO it."

- Erik Qualman

Angel financing – Investments in new business by wealthy individuals or firms known as "business angels."

Assets – The valuable resources or properties and property rights owned by the company. Included might be cash, inventory, equipment and buildings.

Branding – Positioning your business with a marketing image.

Break-even point – The level of sales where profits made from sales equal total costs and expenses.

Broadening the Pond (Burwell term) – Using the ripple effect to manage your growth. Touching people's lives in a positive way.

Capacity – Ability to pay back a loan. Compares the cash flow to the monthly minimum loan payment.

Capital – Money and other assets you would use to start up a business, ownership.

Channel of distribution – The steps in which a product or service moves from start to the consumer. It may be business to business (indirect) or business to consumer (direct).

 Collateral – Securities, evidence of deposit, or other property pledged by a borrower to secure repayment of a loan.

Competition – Business rival for customers or markets. Any company that sells a similar product or service to the same people you want to sell to.

"Cupiding©" (Burwell term) – Connecting businesses and entrepreneurs that share common visions, goals, interests and/or talents.

Demographics – The statistical study of human populations, especially with reference to size and density, distribution, and vital statistics.

Enterprise team – A group, usually from outside the company, that serves as a number of resources. Non-governing paid and non-paid.

Equity – Equity is the owner's investment in the business. Unlike capital, equity is what remains after the liabilities of the company are subtracted from the assets – thus it may be greater or less than the capital invested in the business. Equity investment carries with it a share of ownership and usually a share in the profits, as well as some say in how the business is managed.

Expenditures – How much you spend.

Financial statements – Documents that show your financial situation.

Fiscal year – A 12-month period between settlements of financial accounts.

Fixed costs – Expenses which do not vary with the level of sales, such as loan payments, rent and salaries.

Intrapreneur (Burwell definition) – The creation of value by people and organizations connecting together to implement an idea through the application of innovation, compassion, knowledge, adherence and a willingness to take a risk.

Liabilities – Money that you owe.

Line of credit – An agreement between a commercial bank and a business firm that states the amount of unsecured short-term credit the bank will make available to the borrower.

Logo – Your graphic symbol used for your identity.

Marketing – Creating customers; the process of planning and executing the conception, pricing, promotion, and distribution of ideas, goods, and services to satisfy individual and organizational objectives.

Market busting – Change in marketshare innovation or business growth, but utilizing trend or lifestyle responding. Example: "healthy fast food"

Market niche – A targeted market segment that you determine is not adequately being served by the current competition.

Operating budget – Amount you have budgeted to actually run your business.

Positioning – Marketing strategy used to differentiate products and services from its competitors in the mind of the prospective buyer.

Pricing strategy – Part of marketing is setting prices to cover your expenses, and to make a profit. Types of pricing strategies:

- **Comparative –** Setting the price of its true value and not overpricing, and then establishing an "out of the door price" on what the market will truly buy it at.
- **Penetration –** A strategy of pricing a new product relatively low to encourage wide market acceptance that allows the price to increase later on depending on demand.
- **Prestige Pricing –** Setting a high price to position it as a unique or quality image.
- **Skimming –** This strategy is setting the price of a new product relatively high, then gradually lowering it.

Product life cycle – Four stages of a successful product: Introduction, growth, maturity, and decline.

Profit – Total revenue minus total expenditures.

Psychographics – Used to segment markets. Psychographics is the study of the psychological profiles of individuals. For example, "early adopters" (people who like to be the first to buy something new) have a very different profile from "survivors," people who are barely scraping by and are loathe to buy anything that is not totally familiar to them.

Revenue – An amount of money regularly coming in.

Segmentation – Defining your potential customers by various characteristics such as geographics, demographics, purchasing habits, or lifestyles.

Social enterprise – Any organization, in any sector, that uses earned income strategies to pursue a double bottom line as part of a mixed revenue stream that includes charitable contributions and government sector revenues or subsidies.

Strategic planning – Process of setting organizational objectives, then establishing the strategy and resources to reach these objectives.

SWOT – Marketing analysis on your strengths, weaknesses, opportunities and threats.

Tagline – Phrase that goes with logo that associates your business.

Target market – A group of people with common needs. The most likely potential customers for your business.

Target market (niche market) – Identifying a market segment not adequately served by the competition in which you direct your marketing efforts.

Trend Responder (Burwell term) – Responding to product of services that meet today's current lifestyle.

Undercapitalization – Providing too little capital for the successful operation of the business.

Variable costs – Expenses that fluctuate based on the amount of sales.

Vendors – Suppliers of goods and services to your business

"Believe you can and you're halfway there."

- Theodore Roosevelt